M000086633

Printed in Los Angeles, CA

Book design and layout by Mark Findler
BenchMark Design Co.
www.benchmarkdesignco.com

Editor: Kathi Whitman
In Credible English®
Salt Lake City, UT
www.incredibleenglish.com

First published by Dog Ear Publishing
4011 Vincennes Road
Indianapolis, IN 46268
www.dogearpublishing.net

ISBN: 978-1-4575-4825-3

This book is printed on acid free paper.
Printed in the United States of America

per·pe·tu·i·ty:

An annuity that has no end, or a stream of cash payments that continues forever.

Praise for Craig O'Rourke's
Destination Perpetuity

Destination Perpetuity is an easy-to-read, step-by-step guidebook that introduces the reader to the concept of creating a financially secure future by building a real portfolio. The format of the book is light, fun, and easy to read. Written as a journey, the reader is taken on an expedition on the road to Perpetuity (an annuity without end).

The novice investor will find all the basic concepts and knowledge on everything from the rudimentary language of real estate all the way to the proper way in which to analyze an asset.

The already-seasoned, savvy investor will also appreciate the many tips and real life stories of dos and don'ts as well as the creative concepts of expanding from a single building to a portfolio of properties.

This book should be considered essential reading for anyone serious about creating mailbox income from real estate.

Book Review, September 2015 issue
APARTMENT AGE Magazine
The Voice of Multifamily Housing Since 1917 ©

As a 37-year veteran of the real estate business, I have bought and sold many properties for myself as well as helped hundreds of clients purchase properties. As I was reading Craig O'Rourke's *Destination Perpetuity*, I found myself saying over and over again, "I wish I had this book 37 years ago." This book is a must-have tutorial for anyone wanting to seriously invest in real estate. I highly recommend it.

Jeff Culbertson
Executive Vice President, Southwest Region
National Real Estate Trust

Craig O'Rourke's *Destination Perpetuity* not only addresses key questions on navigating today's complex real estate market, it also drafts a roadmap to success with clear detail as well as step-by-step coaching from one of the industry's recognized leaders. It's the definitive guide on real estate investing, portfolio development, and fundamentally sound business thinking that creates *mailbox income* and asset growth. Craig's overlay of humor makes for an entertaining read. Well done!

Rob Nelson
First Capital Mortgage
Vice President of Production
Radio Host of "Nelson Radio" on Business, Finance,
Real Estate, and Law

Craig O'Rourke's *Destination Perpetuity* is an easy-to-comprehend guide to investing in income property. Written in an amusing fashion and illustrated with relevant, true-life stories, this book will inspire you to begin your journey to the destination of *Perpetuity* —a life free of money anxiety.

This book should occupy a permanent space in the library of anyone who has been curious but inhibited at the prospect of income unit investment. Keep it within an arm's reach!

I want to get a copy to my son and his bride immediately. How I wish I would have had this resource earlier in my life — yet now I am convinced it is not too late.

Betty Graham
President, Previews International
Luxury Real Estate

It is well known that much of the wealth that has been accumulated throughout the world has been generated through the ownership of real estate. This simple, easy-to-read guide for real estate investors provides a great introduction and simplifies the process for those who wish to begin to build their future real estate wealth.

I have known Craig O'Rourke for some time, and I know that the guidance and insights that Craig has put into this book come from many years of personal experience. I am confident that you will find this book to be a great tool as you embark on your journey of real estate investing and wealth building.

Robert K. Foster
President and Chief Operating Officer
Coldwell Banker Greater Los Angeles

Craig O'Rourke's *Destination Perpetuity* should be a must read for all real estate practitioners. It changes the real estate agent to not just a locator of property for purchase, but an estate builder for their clients as well as themselves. It's easy to follow, amusing, and an incredible confidence builder.

It's never too late to plan for the future: for you, for your children, and of course for your grandchildren. Not only is it an easy read, it creates a challenge and so many possibilities for fun while you are making money.

Diane Manns
President of Beverly Hills and Greater Los Angeles
Board of Realtors®

Craig O'Rourke writes a guide, but not just a guide. No presumptions are made, so the reader can have the opportunity to learn 100% of the information, or take the 75% that they may not know. But most important is that there are no guesses or questions left when you are finished with this tome. It says it all, and no one has to feel like they are being re-taught something they already know; instead, they get a new perspective. For sure, this information has never been presented in such a clear and succinct manner. Craig is a genius. At times, I thought maybe he was reading my mind because as a question came to me, the very next paragraph explained it in clear intelligent language with no ambiguities. That may be the key to this book: Nothing is left to chance or presumption. And that is first in education. Craig is a Teacher, and we are respected Students. Well done.

Dr. Jim Lee
Real Estate Investor

As an attorney for over 23 years, I have seen investment trends come and go, and represented good people in the aftermath. The consistent, safe performance of a well-planned real estate portfolio has always stood out.

I continue to hold real estate, and have no intention to ever stop. This inclination is strengthened and now better understood since reading Craig O'Rourke's very readable and thoughtful book. I recommend it strongly, and I plan to always keep an extra copy to hand out to people I care about with questions on investing.

David T. Brown, Esquire
Huskinson and Brown Attorney's at Law
CRB, SFR, CDPE

Craig's book, *Destination Perpetuity*, is essential reading for people who wish to speed up their path to financial freedom by supplementing their retirement account saving with in-come-producing real estate.

Craig's approach to explaining the potential benefits of income-producing real estate is relaxed and easy to digest. It's essential reading for anyone who's eager to take the first step towards being a successful real estate investor.

Barrett Porter, CFP®
Certified Financial Planner / Partner
Abacus Wealth Partners

I find this book so valuable. *Destination Perpetuity* has taken me back to basics and opened my eyes to what was so simple that I had to learn the hard way.

I will recommend my friends already in real estate and those just entering it to buy this book!

Julie Summers
Real Estate Portfolio Investor

Destination Perpetuity is a must read! Craig O'Rourke hit the bull's eye when he wrote this book. I enjoyed it from start to finish. If you want to eliminate fear and empower yourself for independence and success this book provides the tools needed to build your wealth.

Not only is the material easy to understand but also it is jam-packed with important definitions, explanations, checklists, tips, and relevant examples. Investing in income property is a wise decision if you know what you are doing! Craig provides incredible insight for both novice and experienced investors. Unlike many similar how-to guides, this one is crafted with humor, attention to detail, and in-depth analysis, all the while remaining an easy read. I looked forward to every chapter. Craig has made my holiday shopping easier!

Kathy Mehringer
CRB, SFR, CDPE
California Association of Realtors® Director for Life

I would like to acknowledge my friends and colleagues who gave generously of their time, energy, and ideas to help me make this book the very best it could be.

Special thanks to:

Linda & John Black
Karen Bergan
Taya DiCarlo
Denise Feneht
Mark Findler
Anne Marie Gilroy
Richard Hollowell
Xishel Hyde
Shyrl Lorino
Michael O'Hara
Mark Poncher

Most of all, I would like to acknowledge the driving force behind this book: my partner Andrew and our son Tyler, who give meaning and joy to my journey.

This book is dedicated to my parents, Mike and Elaine O'Rourke. It was from their wise investments that I have learned to walk this path. Thanks Mom and Dad.

Table of Contents

Introduction

"A journey of a thousand miles must begin with a single step." - Lao Tzu

I have always seen life as a series of journeys, and one of the most important ones — oftentimes the most poorly planned – is the journey towards financial freedom. When I ask my friends and colleagues when they plan to retire, few if any can give me a plausible timeline. Far too often I hear the same cynical retort, "I'll retire when I'm dead!" Personally, I think that's a bad plan. This book seeks to remedy that mistake.

I am a baby boomer. Born in 1960, I am at the tail end of my generation. For decades, we boomers enjoyed the fruits of a strong economy. Jobs were plentiful, salaries and bonuses seemed solid, and our standard of living was unmatched by previous generations or by our peers around the world. A secure financial life came fairly easy to us boomers; however, partly due to those rather soft times, many of us boomers developed a sense of entitlement. Not good.

Then a few years ago, things began to go south. The dot-com surge went bust, banks failed, the stock market spiraled into a tailspin, and real estate values plummeted. Nervous homeowners turned to their equity credit line checkbooks only to find that false security blanket had been yanked away along with the vanishing equity value of their homes. IRA and 401K accounts that workers had diligently paid into year after year were first bludgeoned by investors fleeing the market and then picked clean by the individuals who had funded them. Jobs began to disappear, and with them went the much-anticipated retirement packages and promised pensions. Families struggled to pay off their underwater, over-leveraged home mortgages. Things went from bad to worse, and suddenly the privileged, bulletproof baby boomers began to notice a taint to the generational silver spoons they had all been sharing. Their sense of entitlement morphed into a sense of dread. As the boomers approached retirement age, stories of senior citizens eating peanut butter sandwiches to save money for their cancer medication began to hit a little too close to home. The ship was sinking, and it didn't matter that everyone was in the same boat; it was every man for himself, and there were few life rafts in sight.

With unemployment in the double digits, baby boomers found themselves suddenly scrambling to compete with younger, better-educated, 20-somethings who would work twice as hard for half as much. It seemed re-entering the work force had become an insurmountable obstacle as experience proved no match for cutting-edge skills. Once casual banter with friends and colleagues over the virtues of a Mercedes versus a BMW shifted to anxious concerns about the cheapest place to retire and tips on how to best avoid outliving one's nest egg.
As all this turmoil raged, my mother sat quietly in a guard-gated community in Manhattan Beach, California, planning a trip to Hawaii for herself, her children, and her grandchildren — all on her own dime. Whenever she went out to dinner,

she would always insist on picking up the check. She was considering buying a new car because her Jaguar was giving her problems. Although she was well aware that the economy in general was bleak, she also knew her personal financials were sound. While the world cringed on the fiscal cliff, she stood on solid bedrock. Now, please understand that my mother is not a wealthy woman. She is, however, well-off and will remain that way, sleeping peacefully at night with the knowledge that her financial position is secure. How was that possible, you may ask, when the rest of the world had suddenly decided that a Starbucks Grande was a frivolous expense and coupon cutting had become a national pastime?

The answer is one simple word: **Perpetuity.**

If you search Wikipedia for the definition, you will find the following:

> *"Perpetuity is an annuity that has no end; or a stream of cash payments that continues forever."*

My mother enjoys a perpetual income from a few properties she and my father invested in many years ago.

My father had worked in sales his entire life and had no retirement set up. Having watched their parent's generation struggle with meager social security checks, my parents decided to create a better life for their retirement years. In their 50s, my mother and father began buying income-producing properties that they knew would fund a safe, secure, long-term retirement for them both. My mother and father enjoyed over 20 years of a financially worry-free retirement because of the passive income from their real estate investments. In the year 2000, my father passed away, and he left this world knowing that his wife of 57 years would never have to worry about money. Additionally, he knew that his children and grandchildren would have solid financial starts, all due to the well-planned stream of perpetual income he and my mother had created decades earlier.

To this day, my mother still lives off the investments she and my father began making in the 1970's. Today, my mother is 95, and if she lives to be 100 or beyond, she knows her finances are stable. She has this financial comfort zone because she has lived with a steady stream of *mailbox income* for over 35 years. She knows that even if she spends every dime in her checking account, more money will come next month.

A friend of my mother's recently said to her, "You are so lucky to have that income." Truth is, luck had nothing to do with it. My father planned ahead and followed a simple set of real estate investment principles. He understood the rules of the road, knew what the hazards were, and avoided them. He also knew how not to be tempted by financial detours. He stayed the course and enjoyed many retirement years of complete, stress-free financial freedom.

Why did my parents and so many other income-producing real estate investors weather the downturn that crushed other forms of retirement plans?

The answer is simple. Income-producing properties purchased wisely continue to provide cash flow in almost any economy. Although real estate values can plummet, income generated from these types of properties typically remains stronger than other types of real estate. Why? It is because they operate like a business rather than strictly a real estate investment. In many markets, rents remained solid, while some rents even went up. This was often the case even though the value of the property went down and the market price of real estate was in a tailspin. Why?

Well, let's look at what happened around 2007. The economy faltered. Businesses cut back or closed down. Jobs disappeared and salaries evaporated. Factories closed, office space shrank, and the newly unemployed could no longer make their mortgage payments. Businesses and homeowners were simply giving the keys to their property back to the bank. Financial institutions were overrun with foreclosures, REOs, and short sales. Every sector of the economy including real estate was hit hard. Well, almost every sector. The exception was the cash flow from income-producing properties.

Rarely did a properly managed apartment building purchased in the right location suffer such a fate. *Why not?* Simple. Everyone needs a place to live. When homeowners handed their keys over to the banks, they became tenants, thereby increasing the demand for rentals. Smart investors who already owned income-producing apartment buildings simply hung onto their properties, and the really smart ones bought even more. The cash flow provided by the tenants gave the investors the ability to continue paying their mortgages and other bills. This is not to say that income-producing properties did not depreciate in value. Most did, and some did so dramatically, but the point is that owners of income-producing properties were better able to weather the economic downturn.

Simply put, properties that generate cash flow hold their value better than other types of real estate in down markets, and the value of these same properties almost always increases at a faster rate and higher percentage when compared to a non-income producing personal residence.

Now, let's take a quick quiz. Don't panic, just four questions:

(Remember this is a workbook, so go ahead and write in it. It will be interesting for you to look back at your notes once you have begun traveling this journey. You may find that your answers sometimes change but most often in a positive way.)

1. **How and when do I plan to retire?**
   (Many people cannot answer this simple question. You need to ask it. Sit with your husband, wife, or life partner and toss this around. The answers or lack of answers may shock you.)

----

2. Where do I want to retire?
This is an important question
because the cost of living in
Paris, France is far greater than
the cost of living in Perris, California.

(Pick at least three destinations, and
then do a Google search to find out what
the median income is for those areas. That will
give you an idea of the cost-of-living differences.)

_____

_____

_____

_____

_____

_____

_____

3. How much money do I need to live on per year?
(Think long and hard on this one.
Do you want to travel? Are you a
car guy? Do you dream of having a
separate closet just for shoes? If
you answered yes to any of these,
you may want to budget for business
class retirement instead of coach.)

_____

_____

_____

_____

_____

_____

_____

4. How long do you think you will live?
   75 – 80 – 85 – 90 – 95 – 100 – 105 – longer?

   (Careful, this is a trick question. Unless you are a great psychic, you have to really second-guess this one. Both of my grandmothers lived into their late 80s, and my mom and her twin sister are going strong at 95. Plan for the long haul, just in case.)

This book will show you step-by-step how to create a stream of perpetual cash flow with income-producing real estate. Most people have a common goal of a financially safe and sound retirement that is comfortable and allows them to live their lives without the fear of outliving their money. Who doesn't want a financial sanctuary where you will find peace of mind — not only for yourself — but also for generations to come? Trust me, you will like *Perpetuity*.

Ninety percent of all millionaires
become so through owning
real estate.

Andrew Carnegie

Chapter 1
Is This a Road I Want to Travel?

A close friend of mine is a successful, certified financial planner and partner in his firm. We respect each other's professional opinions, but we also love to have the occasional sparring session over the topic of investing. We both agree that real estate ownership is an essential strategy for any solid retirement plan. As you might imagine, we never agree on how much real estate is the right amount.

Obviously, there is no scientifically proven correct percentage. My friend feels that a person needs to be wealthy before it makes sense to own a piece of income-producing real estate;

I disagree. I feel you must be financially stable and have a handle on your income vs. debt before purchasing income-producing real estate. From my experiences, I have found that, for most people, becoming wealthy typically includes owning real estate. It is common knowledge that a large portion of the wealth worldwide is in real estate holdings. Clearly, owning real estate and especially income-producing real estate is a key to wealth building — the practice has been around for thousands of years. You don't need to be rich to do it, just very knowledgeable and very aware of the risks involved.

The truth of the matter is that different investment paths exist because different people have different needs and different levels of tolerance. I am a big believer in diversification, and I have a fantastic, fee-only financial planner and a great CPA who guide me with investments other than real estate. I do, however, firmly believe that real estate investments are the best of the best for long-term investors, if planned and operated correctly.

A friend of mine shared a Buddhist saying about the path to spirituality. I do not remember the exact phrase, but I recall it goes something like this:

"Spirituality is like a mountain, there are many paths to the top, Buddhism is but one."

There are many paths to financial freedom; I always advise my clients to look into other forms of investing as well and determine what is right for their individual goals. As I said earlier, this book is written as a journey. Consider this book one of the pathways to financial enlightenment. Income-producing real estate is but one path to financial stability, and it is by no means a simple one, unless of course you have a plan. This book is written not only to explain the basic mechanics of real estate investing, but also to help you decide if this path is the right one for you. Achieving financial freedom requires both short and long-term commitments. You must plot a course, pay attention to the map, avoid detours, and most importantly, learn the rules of the road. Pitfalls on this journey can result in costly mistakes, but through the guidance in this book, you can avoid many of the usual bumps, wrong turns, and dead ends. Good planning is the key to success.

To find out if real estate investing is right for you, take a thoughtful read through these next few pages. Also, if you come across words or phrases that are foreign to you, *Chapter 2: Learning the Lingo* will help with unfamiliar vocabulary.

Before we begin, let's start off with some basic Q and A and tackle these fears one by one:

If income-producing real estate is such a good investment, why isn't everyone doing it?

Great question. I have two answers.

The first is the simplest: **It's not easy.** But nothing worthwhile is. So if you are not willing to put in a little hard work, give this book to someone who is enthusiastic to learn something new. The learning curve is not difficult, but it will take time and dedication.

Now the more complicated answer: **Fear.** Anxiety abounds, especially when money is involved. It's a road many are afraid to travel. People think it is too complicated, too expensive, and too much of a hassle.

If either of these answers is holding you back, stop worrying. You are not alone. You are holding the map in your hands. The course has been plotted for you. All you have to do is follow along. After reading this book, you will know if this path is right for you or not.

I could never afford to buy an apartment building.

Although the real estate market took a beating a few years ago, income-producing properties did not see an equivalent reduction in value. Why did income-producing properties hold a better percentage of value? Simple. Owning property of any type costs you money every month. Mortgage, taxes, insurance, and maintenance are all on you. When the economy melted down and jobs were lost, monthly paychecks were disappearing and so did the ability to continue paying all those bills. Unlike your home, income-producing properties create a perpetual cash flow. If you planned your purchase properly, your tenants should be continuing to pay your property bills (mortgage, taxes, insurance, maintenance, etc.) via their rent checks. If a tenant fails to pay, another tenant is waiting to take over and continue making your payments. Income-producing real estate is a business. If you understand what to buy, how to buy, and how to manage your property, your cash flow continues regardless of most economic downturns.

As you read through this book, most of the examples are based on my own or my clients' experiences. I work in the Southern California market, and the dollar amounts I discuss may seem outrageously high if you are living in another part of the planet, but don't think you need to have millions to get on board the cash flow train. For example, I know of an investor that makes her living in a college town in Missouri. She is paying her bills with the rental income from five small houses valued at about $100,000 each. She lives in the smallest one, rents out the one next door via Airbnb, and has tenants in the other three. She is not wealthy; however, she enjoys a comfortable, predictable income and can afford to travel often.

One of my best deals came from a $5,000 initial investment I made with two other partners. It was a small, single-family home that we held for a few years and then traded via a 1031 tax exchange for a duplex. After a few more years, we traded the duplex into a multifamily apartment building. My point is that you don't have to be rich, but you do have to be smart, patient, and willing to work hard.

It's too late to buy. I missed the bottom.

If you don't already own real estate, you might be feeling like you missed the boat. The market is constantly in flux, so stop whining and get on board! Forget about the bragging rights of buying at the bottom. Remember this is a long journey, and the bottom of the market continually resets. Real estate grows over time. The market is fluid; the value of a property represents a moment in time. Cyclical markets will always produce new highs and new lows. The key is to get in and stay in. Over time, real estate delivers. In the 1950s, people thought they missed the bottom of the market in the 1940s. That story repeats itself decade after decade. Even if you had the misfortune of buying real estate at the top of the market just before a crash, the market will correct itself over time and deliver you a valuable property. Don't get me wrong, timing is important, but real estate is very forgiving. Even if your timing is off, be patient, and the market will reward you over time — **if** you have followed the rules of the road.

Think of real estate investment as long term. Improvements are made, rents go up, properties burn down, and areas become blighted and are later revitalized. The point is that everything changes. The real estate market goes through cycles. There have been many *top* and *bottom* phases, and there will be many more. Hindsight will always allow you to say, "That was the time to buy!"

The reality of timing is that most every real estate investor second-guesses timing with questions like:

- Is the economy solid?
- Should I wait a year?
- What will happen with my job?
- Is this the right area?

All of these are valid concerns and ones you should consider; however, at some point in time, every investment — be it in real estate or another asset — will involve some type of risk when deciding to move forward. One of the reasons I like real estate so much is that it is typically the most forgiving when it comes to mistakes.

Journeys require direction and information. If you were heading out of town on a ski vacation, you would most likely want to know the snow pack, weather conditions, and hotel room availability before hitting the road. For the purpose of our journey, I have highlighted 12 issues that first-time real estate investors tend to worry about when embarking on this path. Let's break down these issues one by one and try to also break down any fears you might have.

Issue #1: When is the right time to buy?

The time to get in is when you see an opportunity. A good real estate agent understands the area and the local economy and can advise you on timing. I remember my father lamenting about having waited until the 1970s to buy. "I wish I had bought in the '60s. I really missed the market," he said. Today, it's easy to see how wrong he was. One of the properties he purchased was recently appraised for 20 times the original purchase price. That is not what I call missing the market.

In my own case, I recently purchased an eight-unit building at 4.5 percent interest. That market had seen a huge upswing, and some investors had lamented that they missed the bottom. My decision to purchase was not based on buying at the bottom to get the best deal; my decision was based on a deal that made sound economic sense. I conservatively anticipate that the building will appreciate at about 3 to 5 percent annually as California real estate typically does. But even if the naysayers were correct and the market faltered downward for a few years with little or no appreciation or even negative appreciation, I would not be concerned. I invest for the long haul and look for properties that will weather financial downturns. A big part of my decision to purchase this particular property was based on my strong belief that inflation is coming and with it higher rents. Since I have a locked-in interest rate, my monthly payment stays the same, but the higher rents will in turn increase cash flow, making the property more valuable as rents increase with rising inflation. Since I plan to hold the building long term, the potential ups and downs of real estate values are not as much of a concern as the cash flow aspect, which I believe should be very solid.

Issue #2: What if my property loses value?

Let's be clear; income-producing real estate is not exempt from devaluation. Believe me, we income-producing property owners took our hits with beaten-down equity, but those of us who stayed on the journey found the downturn of values coupled with decade-low interest rates to be an amazing opportunity. With low interest rates, inflation then becomes your welcome travel partner on the road to financial freedom. When you buy a fixed mortgage, you have fixed your payment. When inflation comes, as it always does, owners of income-producing properties are to some extent insulated from an inflating economy and may even profit from it. Why? Your rents go up, but your mortgage stays the same. Bottom line is that your cash flow increases year after year. Inflation? Bring it on!

Issue #3: How much appreciation can I count on?

None. Your property will appreciate, and your real estate agent can show you historical data about how a certain type of building in a certain area has appreciated in the past, but this book is not about predicting future appreciation. History and inflation tell us your property will appreciate; however, you cannot count on a number; you can only utilize educated guesses. Remember, appreciation is a by-product of demand and an excellent consequence of your income-producing real estate investment. But if you are looking to make fast money on appreciation, this may not be the path for you to take. This book is about the journey of acquiring assets to hold long term. Many a real estate investor has gotten into financial hot water by betting heavily and trying to *time* a pop in the market. I'm not saying it can't be done, but that's not the goal I am setting forth. Think of appreciation as a bonus and often times an extremely lucrative one.

Even if property has been appreciating at a steady 3 to 5 percent rate for a number of years, counting on a certain rate to continue is an extremely risky proposition. It can cause you to overpay for properties, expecting to realize the difference at sale from appreciation. When you buy income-producing real estate, do it with the long haul in mind. Don't let the periodic ups and downs of real estate values distract your attention from your goal: long-term, steady cash flow.

Issue #4: It's too much of a hassle to watch over an investment property.

Not to worry. If you don't have the time or inclination to watch over your property, you can hire a property manager. The pros, cons, and costs of property management should be discussed with your real estate agent and financial advisor. If property management is the way for you to go, the cost should be built into your budget as a monthly expense before you even consider making an initial offer on a property. Trained professionals will handle the bills, maintenance, advertising, and late rents. With the right property management team in place, all you should have to do is check in with your manager to review the books. You make the big-picture decisions, like when to freshen up the paint or re-landscape, and then let the property manager tend to the day-to-day details.

Your only other concern should be depositing the distribution checks your property manager sends you after all the bills are paid. That first deposit is a small step towards *Perpetuity*, and believe me when I say it will make you smile every time you see that check in the mailbox, hence the term, *mailbox income.*

Issue #5: Property managers cost too much.

If you want to make even more money, you can do so by cutting the property management company out of the equation. You will enjoy collecting an additional 5-12 percent of income annually. But, be careful with this one. Property management sounds easier than it is, and a good property manager may actually save you money.

Ask yourself a few simple questions to determine if you should or should not manage your own building.

Are you qualified? Before answering this one, run through these scenarios in your mind:

- Are you willing to handle an emergency plumbing call at 3:00 am?

- Run credit checks?

- Meet the handyman on site for a bid?

- Supervise and verify that the handyman's work is complete and meets local codes.

If you answered no to any of these questions, you have your answer; however, if you answered yes, here is your next test.

What is your time worth?

- Depending on the size of your portfolio, you could be taking on a full-time job.

- Interview potential property managers to determine how much they will charge and how many hours per week or month they would be spending on managing your property. Then, determine if you have that much free time and if it is worth that dollar amount.

Really? At what age are you planning on retiring? 60? 65? 70?

Find properties with decent cash flow, and rather than taking the proceeds now, use that cash flow to pay down the note. A property with a good cash flow can often be paid off years before the 30-year note comes due. Do the math, and map out what annual dollar amount it will take to get the mortgage paid off in 15 years. If you're 50 when you purchase, a paid-for building at 65 will look really appealing.

Now, let's look at the really big question. How long are you planning on living? 75 years? 80? 100? If you retire at 65 and live to 90, that's 25 years of day-to-day expenses, not to mention the cost of elder health care. Counting on Social Security? Not a good idea.

Now, take a moment and ponder this not-fun fact, courtesy of Northwest Mutual's *Planning and Progress Study 2013:*

> 56 percent of Americans say they are financially
> prepared to live to age 75, yet 10 percent expect to
> work into their 80s.

Let's stop here for a second. Only 56 percent of Americans say they are financially prepared to live to age 75? As I write this, I am a 53-year-old male. I don't smoke; I have no life-threatening diseases; I get check-ups regularly; and I drink only in moderation. Based on all that data, the Census Bureau generously gives me 23 more years to live. Now with those same stats but swapping genders, you 53-year-old ladies get an extra 3 years. That sounds great, but only if you have two things: your health and some cash flow. You will need to read a different book to get advice on the health part, but you have come to the right place to learn how to keep constantly putting dollars in your pocket. What happens to all those Americans who planned finances for 75 and keep living until 105? If you are lucky enough to have children and grandchildren, the last thing you will want is to burden them with grandpa and grandma moving in. Worse yet, what happens if you have no family? Old, broke, and no family is a really bad scenario. Let's cure one of these issues. Keep your money rolling, and no matter what happens, dependable cash flow will make it smoother.

Enough with the doom and gloom, let's talk about some fun stuff. Where is all the money coming from to pay for your Alaskan cruise, wine tasting weekends in Sonoma and hang gliding lessons? What about your spouse, your children, and your grandchildren? Don't you want to leave them as secure as possible? Still think you're too old to start? Think again. And remember that the real estate market is cyclical. Don't fret over having missed the boat, but jump on the next one, and the guy behind you who waits on the dock will most likely feel he is the one who missed the boat. Until we colonize the moon, we are fresh out of new land. Grab it while you can.

Issue #7: My stockbroker told me real estate is not right for me.

He might be right, but you must always consider the source. Real estate is certainly not for everyone. Stockbrokers typically want to sell you stock, and real estate agents want to sell you real estate. Go to a neutral party. Ask your CPA or financial planner. And while you are at it, ask anyone who owns income-producing property. Information is power, so ask others who have journeyed before you. Make a list of people you know who live in *Perpetuity*, and ask them what path they followed to get there. Two words you will almost certainly hear will be *real estate*.

Issue #8: Which is better: A fixed or variable loan?

When a loan is fixed for its entire term, it will be fixed at the then-prevailing market interest rate, plus or minus a spread that is unique to the individual borrower and property. A variable interest rate loan is one in which the interest rate on the outstanding balance varies as market interest rates change. As a result, your payments will vary as well. Generally speaking, if interest rates are relatively low, and you intend to hold on to property long term, then it will be better to lock in your loan at that fixed rate. Depending on the terms of your agreement, your interest rate on the new loan will remain fixed, even if interest rates climb to higher levels. On the other hand, if you expect rates to remain constant or decline, then it might be better to have a variable rate loan. As interest rates fall, so will the interest rate on your loan, which will in turn lower your monthly mortgage. But be careful with this one, eventually rates will go up.

Variable interest rates are appealing because they are often offered at a much lower rate, and that low rate is typically a fixed rate for anywhere from 1–10 years. If you don't plan on holding the property long term, a variable interest rate may be the ticket. However, keep in mind that life changes and you want to be ready for that curve in the road you didn't see coming. Low fixed-interest rates are inexpensive travel insurance for your journey.

Be careful here. Variable rates can sink the ship. Ultimately, you will want to lock the rate. When interest rates rise, it can happen rapidly and a point or two increase in your rate can promptly lessen or even wipe out your cash flow. Interest rates fixed at a low rate can be your insurance for long-term cash flow.

Remember you are not just buying a property; you are buying a payment. When you throw the dice with a variable rate, your investment is at the mercy of economic conditions. If rates go up, you could lose not only your desired retirement, but also your initial investment as well. Be very careful with variable interest rates. It can be like a side trip to Vegas that spirals out of control. Throw the dice at the craps table, not with your investment.

By now, you know I like fixed rates. Here's why. Fixed interest rate loans are loans in which the interest rate charged remains fixed for that loan's entire term, regardless of what happens to the market price of interest rates. This will result in your mortgage payments being the same over the entire term of the loan. The nice thing about a fixed rate is that inflation becomes your happy travel companion. Everything variable goes up over time, including the rent you are charging. If you have a fixed-rate, your monthly mortgage payments will stay the same, so as rents go up, so does your income. Bottom line is that your rate of return can increase dramatically via inflation. Whether a fixed-rate loan is better for you or not will depend on the interest rate environment when the loan is taken out and on the duration of the loan. Remember that rates change constantly. If you acquire a variable rate and you don't have a prepayment penalty, you can more comfortably take advantage of the market when and if rates drop, thereby further increasing your cash flow. Be careful here; this can make or break your investment.

Issue #9: What will my return be?

The anticipated return on your investment can be calculated using a variety of methods. Typically, the capitalization rate or gross rent multiplier is utilized to determine an approximate return. If you are unfamiliar with these terms, chapter 2 will be of great help to you. There are a variety of ways to look at an income-producing property, and those will be discussed later in the book. However, as long as the information supplied is accurate, you can get a good idea about the cash flow on which your newly acquired property will operate by simply inserting your purchase-specific costs. Of course, that is only one source of income. As discussed earlier, appreciation can often be your most lucrative wealth-building tool; however, be careful not to take a detour to the equity ATM. It's a tempting stop to make, but the equity you build is arguably the most important tool in growing your retirement portfolio, so don't get derailed at this juncture. Short of a true emergency, you should leave your equity alone with one single exception: Buying more property that increases your portfolio and improves your cash flow. This is known as leveraging, and will be discussed in further detail when we get to *Chapter 9: Building Your Portfolio.*

Issue #10: What will my costs be?

It takes money to make money, and if you are not willing or able to shell out some cash, this may not be your path. Every property is unique and will require you, your real estate agent,

CPA, and financial advisor to thoroughly review the proposed transaction and related cost vs. return to determine if the property will meet your financial expectations. Finding the right real estate agent and CPA are of paramount importance in making sure you get the numbers right. (More on this in *Chapter 3: Choosing Your Travel Companions*.)

Let's start with the basic costs to keep in mind. I have broken them into two categories: One-time expenses and re-occurring expenses.

One-Time Expenses

Down Payment — This is typically the biggest dollar amount for a buyer to cough up. Generally, lenders want a minimum of 20 percent down for most real estate transactions; however, when you are looking at non-owner occupied, income-producing properties, the lender will often want to see anywhere from 20–40 percent down depending on multiple factors. If you are a first time buyer, consider creating a partnership. That's how I started.

TRAVEL TIP

With five units, the game changes. You will need to get a commercial loan, and depending on the financial institution's requirements and your credit rating, your debt-to-income ratio, and the property's cash flow history, you may be asked to pay a significantly higher down payment. Bottom-line: four or less income-producing units are much easier to finance and generally the preferred place for a new landlord to start in the business.

Escrow — Think of escrow as a neutral third party. The escrow company and the escrow officer have no real power in the transaction. Escrow simply takes instructions from both parties via the purchase agreement and then creates a set of escrow instructions to help keep track of the transaction and paperwork. If you live in an escrow state, the escrow officer will process the escrow paperwork in accordance with the escrow instructions. When all conditions required in the escrow are achieved, the escrow will be closed. Escrow fees are based on the dollar amount of the sale and can vary from one escrow company to another. Keep in mind that not all states use escrow companies; some use attorneys instead.

Lender Fees — (also called points) Don't be fooled by no-point loans. You are not getting the loan for free, so you will want to find out up front from your lender what the fees will be. Ask for a loan estimate before signing off.

Physical Inspection — The cost of a physical inspection of your proposed property is arguably the most important investment you can make into a property you don't yet own. Think of a physical inspection as a sort of insurance policy. The seller and the sellers agent are required to disclose every negative issue and material fact potentially affecting the value of the property; however, some owners are not always forthcoming with information they feel might jeopardize the sale. Also, there may very well be issues lurking that are completely unknown to the seller. For these two reasons, a physical inspection is a must-do expense.

Real Estate Brokerage Commissions — Real estate brokerage fees are almost always paid for exclusively by the seller. If you are a buyer or a seller, your agent is working for free until the transaction closes. Keep that in mind, and be respectful of the agent's time and energies.

Title — These fees can vary depending on the type of policy you choose. Find out up front from your title agent what the costs will likely be. Your real estate agent can help you review title charges to make sure you are purchasing the proper coverage and paying an appropriate market rate.

Re-Occurring Fees

Maintenance — Repairs are consistently needed to keep your property in prime shape to retain your current tenancy and to attract new tenants when vacancies occur. Maintenance should be ongoing and can be costly at times.

You will need to fund and maintain a bank account for ongoing and emergency maintenance. If you follow the rules of the road, you will factor in your maintenance fees before making an offer on a property. Do your homework, and avoid the unexpected as much as possible with a reasonable maintenance fund.

In *Chapter 4: Mapping Out Your Journey,* you will find a workbook section to help you keep track of good maintenance providers. I highly recommend you take a few minutes on your journey to stop and write down any referrals you get for maintenance. Once you own the building, ongoing maintenance will be one of your best opportunities to secure your cash flow and ensure the overall value of your property, thereby preserving your original investment and growing your future equity. I personally like to have a minimum of six months' expenses in an interest-bearing *rainy day* account on hand and easily accessible. If the building is in a state of disrepair, you might want at least 12 months' expenses put in reserve.

Property Management — Good property managers are worth their weight in gold, and bad ones are like lead weights that can sink the ship. Property managers typically charge anywhere from 5–12 percent of the gross rents collected. This sounds like a lot, but if they are doing their job right, they will be protecting and growing your investment, allowing you more time to focus on what you want to do in life. Time is valuable; believe me, the cost of a good property manager is money well spent.

The Unforeseen — Life happens. Trees fall on roofs, windows break, properties burn to the ground, and people sue each other. Insurance can cover most of the unforeseen but not everything. If you passed on the idea of six months  of expenses for maintenance, at least have a maintenance fund with a minimum of three months' expenses. Trust me, this is a handy thing to have in your back pocket, just in case. Now, before you run away clutching your wallet, remember that with the exception of the unforeseen, you and your agent should have accurately estimated all the costs involved prior to writing an offer on the property. The majority, if not all of these expenses, can and should be cross-referenced with the books and records of the seller during your due-diligence period. Again, you will need to carefully review the numbers with your real estate agent, your CPA, your financial planner, and your lender. This is a business decision. It costs money to make money. Don't be afraid of spending a little money to create a life-long income stream that can last for generations to follow.

It's a long road. Make no mistake: this takes time. Where you invest and the time and money you are willing to invest will greatly affect the length of time it takes to arrive in *Perpetuity*. And even once you get there, it is not a free ride. Even if you have an ace property management team and a building with a low vacancy rate, it's still an ongoing business. You will need to be involved in some level in running it. However, if you do it right, you will find that your time commitment will be minimal and well worth the amount of energy expended in relationship to the cash flow returned.

Issue #11: Do I need a property warranty policy?

A property warranty policy, also known as a *Home Warranty*, is usually requested from the buyer on a property to cover the unforeseen. It's like an insurance policy, but the scope is rather limited, and not all income-producing properties qualify for coverage. Most homebuyers get one on their personal residence, but often investors overlook this step when it comes to income-producing properties. Think of it like this: If you have a home warranty policy that covers the three toilets in your home, wouldn't you want a similar policy covering the 30 toilets in your apartment building? A property warranty is not a warranty at all, but rather a property service contract. A good property warranty policy will often cover the repair and or replacement costs of appliances as well as major systems, such as heating and cooling, and possibly other components of a property, structural or otherwise.

The good news about property warranties is that sellers are typically willing to pay for a one-year policy as part of the sale. The insurance is typically inexpensive compared to the other costs of sale, and a property warranty policy helps the seller mitigate some potential liabilities after the close of sale. If you do get a policy on your property, read the fine print carefully, and make sure you are getting the right policy for your property. Requesting a warranty policy from the seller can be made with the initial offer. Make certain that the dollar amount you request is sufficient to cover the particular requirements of the property you are purchasing. Take the time to read the warranty company's contract, and make sure your specific concerns are addressed in their policy. Some companies offer extended roof coverage; others do not. Some even offer deep discounts on new or replacement appliances. Know your property, and know your policy. Ask your agent for the phone number of the warranty company representative. Do a little homework, and you might just save yourself thousands of dollars down the road.

Issue #12: Won't it be hard to get my money back
          out of real estate if I need quick access
          to equity?

This is sometimes true. Real estate transactions are designed to move slowly. If you decide to sell your property, prepare to be patient. It takes time to choose a real estate agent. Then, it takes time to determine market value. Once that is done, the marketing phase of a listing takes place. It is not unusual for a property to stay on the market for weeks, if not months. The loan process can be arduous and delay closings sometimes for days, weeks, or even months past the agreed-upon closing date.

There are, however, other alternatives to selling the property. If you do not need to access all the building's equity, you may be able to pull money out by adding a second mortgage or line of credit. You must have a good credit score, a good debt-to-income ratio, and a solid amount of equity in the property. This process can also take weeks or even months; however, it can be much less time-consuming than a sale, and you will still retain the asset in your portfolio.

If these questions and issue haven't yet scared you off, you are most likely a good candidate for the road trip to financial freedom; keep reading.

TRAVEL
TIP

There is not much that happens fast with real estate; remember to pack your patience before beginning this journey.

Several years ago, I met a young couple, Bill and Ann. They were interested in buying their first home, but were hesitant about using all of their savings. Bill was a city employee, and Ann was a schoolteacher. They had great credit scores and had saved a sufficient amount for a down payment, but not much more. They were newly married and planned on starting a family in a few years. Although they both had stable jobs, they were limited in their chosen careers as to how much money they could actually earn. Their concern was they did not want to be *house-poor*, a term commonly used to define someone that spends so much on their mortgage, they have little or no money left for savings or other non-essential expenses.

I recommended to Bill and Ann that they consider buying income-producing property as their first purchase. I explained that if they purchased a duplex instead of a single-family home, they could live in one half and rent out the other half. Since the rental income would offset a large portion of their mortgage, they would still be invested in real estate without feeling *house-poor* at the end of each month.

Bill and Ann took my advice and purchased a duplex. They were thrilled with the investment; three years later, they sold it for a sizable profit and purchased a triplex, living in one unit and renting out the other two. Four years after that, Bill and Ann started a family and decided to move into a single-family home. The real estate market had seen solid growth in that time frame. Bill and Ann refinanced the triplex, using cash from their newly acquired equity to purchase their new home, while still maintaining cash flow from their triplex. A decade later, Bill and Ann had two children, two dogs, two triplexes, a duplex, three single-family homes, and an eight-unit apartment building.

I recently received a voicemail from Bill that said the following:

> "Hi Craig! I just called to say thank you. I am sitting on my 40-foot Hatteras pulling out of my boat dock and looking back at my wonderful home. Ann and I would have never been able to have this life if we had not listened to you. Thank you."

Ann and Bill stayed the course. They followed all the rules of the road, and they found their way to *Perpetuity*. You can too. Let's get started.

Rules of the Road

Rule #1

Patience.

Don't wait to buy real estate.
Buy real estate and wait.

John Jacob Astor

Chapter 2
Learning The Language

"The limits of my language mean the limits of my world." – Ludwig Wittgenstein

As with any journey, it helps to know how to speak the local lingo. This chapter contains a few key words for you to add to your vocabulary that will help you to better understand the language and concepts used by the locals who call *Perpetuity* home. As you come to grasp the meaning of the new words, you will also begin to understand that many of these words act as guideposts by which to measure the risk and reward of each potential property along your journey.

Because you will likely want to come back to these terms and their explanations from time to time, I have listed them in alphabetical order to make them easier to access. As a result, there will be times when the explanation for one term includes terms that are defined later in the list.

Real estate agents, lenders, and escrow officers toss around terms with which you need to become familiar. Different methods of analyzing income exist because different investors have different goals. This section is for the true novice: first-timer investors. Astute buyers may want to skip to *Chapter 3: Choosing Your Travel Partners*. For the rest of us, let's get started.

Appraisal

Simply put, appraisal is the process of assigning a dollar value to real property. The term is self-explanatory, but the process is far from simple. Keep in mind that an appraisal is an opinion of value at a moment in time. Also, bear in mind that every property is distinct, and these distinctions affect property value. Cash flow, location, deferred maintenance, amenities, rental history, and vacancy factor all come into play as an appraiser analyzes the merits and deficiencies of each property. Perhaps the most important factor in an appraisal is the recent sales activity, also known as comparables (or more commonly as *the comps*). This is the historical data appraisers and banks scrutinize before assigning a valuation to a property.

When the appraiser prepares the official appraisal to be presented to the lending institution, he/she will only include the recently closed comparable sales for the written report. A good appraiser will look at the market as a whole and should be considering all market activity, which includes properties for which sales are pending (under contract) and properties currently available. Ultimately, however, it is the closed sales that are the main component of the final evaluation.

Keep in mind that appraisals are based on an opinion of value. If the property you want to buy does not appraise for what you expect, you can challenge the appraisal, indicating that you disagree with that particular appraiser's property evaluation. The lending institution then has the option to use the appraisal or re-evaluate the file and assign a different appraiser. Remember that the appraisal is based on recently closed sales; in a rapidly appreciating market, recently closed sales are often considered a lagging indicator of the market. Keep this in mind if you want to argue for a reevaluation of an appraisal.

Appraiser

If you are getting a loan on your property, the appraiser will be working for the lending institution, and his or her job is to determine a property's fair market value. The appraiser comes to the appraised value based a great deal on comparable, recently closed sales as well as the rent rolls and expenses of the subject property, the location, condition, etc.

If you are not getting a loan, you can and should still use an appraiser if you have any question about the value of the property you are considering purchasing. There are many qualified independent appraisers available. Your real estate agent should be able to supply you with referrals.

Appreciation

Simply put, appreciation is the increase in property value due to changes in market conditions, inflation, and supply and demand.

Adjustable Rate Mortgage /ARM

An ARM is a type of mortgage in which the interest changes periodically based on a predetermined index. ARMs are generally fixed for the first three, five, seven, or ten years and then most often adjusted annually with a pre-set maximum.

In many cases, ARMs have limits on how high and sometimes how low the interest rate can go. These *caps* vary from loan to loan. Typically, they adjust annually, but some can adjust quarterly or monthly.

Here is an example:

> For easy numbers, let's go with a $100,000 ARM loan. The interest rate is the prime rate plus 5% with a maximum of 10%. If the prime rate is 3%, then the borrower's interest rate is 8% (5% + 3%), and the monthly payment would be $733.77. But if the prime rate increases to 4%, then the loan's interest rate resets to 9% (5% + 4%), and the payment increases to $804.63.

Amortization / Amortized

Most loan payments consist of two parts: A portion applied to pay the accruing interest on a loan and the remainder applied to the principal. As payments are made, the interest portion of your loan balance decreases as the loan balance also decreases. The amount applied to principal increases, allowing the loan to be paid off or more specifically, *fully amortized.*

Annual Percentage Rate / APR

The APR is not the note rate on your loan. It is a value created according to a government formula, which is intended to reflect the true annual cost of borrowing, expressed as a percentage. Here is the basic formula: Deduct the closing costs from your loan amount; then, using your actual loan payment, calculate what the interest rate would be on this amount instead of your actual loan amount. You will come up with a number close to the APR. Because you are using the same payment on a smaller amount, the APR is always higher than the actual note rate on your loan.

The annual percentage rate includes loan fees and the compound interest rate during the year.

Balloon Mortgage / Balloon Payment

A mortgage loan requires that the remaining principal balance be paid at a specific point in time. These loans typically have lower monthly payments. The loan is typically amortized as if it would be paid over a 30-year period; however, the term can vary from 1 to 25 years for the entire remaining balance to be paid. That final payment is known as the *balloon payment.* These loans are often used by buyers who are not planning on holding the subject property beyond the balloon payment's final payment date.

Books and Records

Owning income-producing real estate is a business, and good records need to be kept. You will hear the term "books and records" regarding the cash flow and expenses of the property. Review these carefully and ask your agent to review as well. A good realtor should be able to determine how accurate the records seem.

TRAVEL TIP *Some people keep two sets of books, so if you are unsure of the books, ask to see the seller's tax returns to cross reference with the records presented.*

Capitalization / Cap Rate

The cap rate assumes the full value of the property when calculating return. The cap rate is the ratio between the net operating income produced by an investment property and its capital cost (the original price paid to buy the property or alternatively, the property's current market value). Keep in mind that the cap rate does not factor in mortgage, principal, or interest.

The rate is calculated with a simple formula:

> Annual Net Operating Income (NOI) / Purchase Price or Value of the Property = Cap Rate

For example:

> NOI $150,000 /Purchase Price $2,000,000 = 7.5% Cap Rate

Both the cap rate and the gross rent multiplier (GRM), which is described later in this chapter, are fluid and will change with the market. If, for example, your building appreciates in value or your rents or expenses change, the GRM and the cap rate will also change accordingly.

Look for high cap rates and low gross rent multipliers (GRMs) to maximize cash flow. Keep in mind there is no set formula for a high cap rate or low GRM. The value assigned to cap rates and GRMs is specific to many factors, not the least of which is the area. You cannot compare cap rates in rural Ohio to cap rates in Time Square. Look to your agent for what is the right cap rate or GRM in your market.

Closing Costs

Closing fees, also called *settlement costs*, cover almost every expense associated with your property purchase. Closing costs vary widely depending on numerous factors. Most closing costs are calculated as a percentage of the sale price and are typically much higher for a seller than a buyer. Each transaction is unique, so be mindful of your closing costs and discuss them with your real estate agent, lender, escrow officer, or attorney.

Examples of common closing fees include:

- **Running your credit report**
- **Loan origination** (charge for processing the loan paperwork)
- **Escrow**
- **Notary**

- **Attorney** (primarily used in non-escrow states)

- **Real estate brokerage** (typically paid by the seller)

- **Required or requested inspections**

- **Discount points** (fees you pay in exchange for a lower interest rate)

- **Appraisal**

- **Survey** (not always required)

- **Title insurance** (which protects the lender and borrower in case the title isn't clear)

- **Title search** (which covers a background check on the title to make sure there aren't things such as unpaid mortgages or tax liens or other types of liens on the property)

- **Pest inspection/extermination**

- **Recording** (which is paid to a city or county in exchange for recording the new land records)

- **Underwriting** (which covers the cost of evaluating a mortgage loan application)

TRAVEL TIP

Junk fees are charges assessed at the closing of a loan that go to the originator, lender, escrow, or title company. These fees are often hidden in the mortgage documents. Junk fees may or may not pay for an actual service to the borrower. Some fees that may be considered junk fees include settlement fees, sign-up fees, underwriting fees, funding fees, translation fees, and messenger fees. Review the settlement statement with your realtor well before closing and challenge any fee you feel is inappropriate.

Closing Disclosure

The *Closing Disclosure* is designed to provide disclosures that will be helpful to consumers in understanding all of the costs of the transaction. The *Closing Disclosure* must be provided to consumers three business days before they close the loan.

Contingency Period / Contingency Removal

A contingency period is also commonly known as a *due-diligence* period. This is the buyer's opportunity to investigate the proposed property within a specified time frame and uncover defects with the physical condition of the property. Books and records are also reviewed and approved or questioned within this same time frame. If all of the physical inspections, books, records, and disclosures are verified and approved, this is known as *contingency removal*, meaning that the contractual contingency to cancel the transaction has been reviewed and lifted. Real estate transactions that include a loan will also have a loan contingency period. Loan contingency periods tend to be the longest and most involved for the buyer.

TRAVEL

TIP

Most often, contingency periods run between 14 to 21 days; however, large buildings with multiple tenants or properties with complicated due-diligence concerns can result in much longer contingency periods. The exact time frame will be negotiated along with the other terms of the proposed purchase prior to signing a purchase contract.

Depreciation

Depreciation refers to the loss in value of a property over time due to physical deterioration, age, and basic wear and tear resulting from normal use. Depreciation is treated as an expense on your taxes. Keep in mind that depreciation can only be used in reference to the structure. While the building will deteriorate over time and eventually need to be replaced, the land will not.

The time frame for deducting depreciation for investment or commercial property is 39 years. Using a straight-line depreciation method for a commercial property costing $2 million dollars, for example, you would receive an annual deduction of $51,282 ($2M / 39 = $51,282). Your annual net income is thereby reduced by that amount for tax purposes, which may reduce the amount of taxes you owe to the IRS.

TRAVEL TIP

IRS rules change, so make sure you double check all tax-related information with your trusted CPA. Don't get advice on taxes from a friend or even your real estate agent. When you think taxes, think CPA.

Down Payment

A down payment is part of the purchase price of a property that the buyer pays in cash. There is no set down payment; however, a down payment is typically between 20 – 40 percent of the purchase price for most income-producing properties.

Dual Agency

This term refers to both buyer and seller being represented by the same brokerage and often times the same agent.

The practice of dual agency is acceptable; however, the brokerage is tasked with a fiduciary duty to both buyer and seller. Before entering into a dual agency, ask your broker how he or she will be able to provide a fiduciary for both you and the other side at the same time.

Due-Diligence Period

The due-diligence period is a time frame that will be negotiated between buyer and seller along with all other contractual points before a deal is agreed to. Most due-diligence time frames run approximately 2 to 3 weeks; however, this time frame can be shortened to a matter of a few days or stretched out for several months. The due-diligence time frame allows the potential buyer to review everything material to the property under contract. Within this time frame, the seller and the seller's broker are required to release any and all material knowledge they have about the condition of the property, issues with the surrounding area, and accurate books and records. This time frame period is the buyer's opportunity to dig deep and find out everything possible about the potential purchase before releasing contingencies.

If a seller or broker withholds information that could affect the value of the property, the seller could face a potential lawsuit, and the broker would risk the same along with the potential suspension or revocation on his or her license.

Estoppels

An estoppel provides information about the lease. This information is provided by the tenants. This document should be compared to the leases provided by the owner. Any discrepancy in the two documents should be addressed and resolved before the end of the due-diligence period.

Evictions

Eviction is the removal of a tenant from a rental property by the landlord. Depending on the laws of the local jurisdiction, eviction may also be known as unlawful detainer, summary possession, summary dispossess, forcible detainer, ejectment, and repossession, among other terms.

Evictions are difficult for all parties, but keep in mind that your income-producing property is a business, and you will need to run it as such. If one of your tenants falls behind in the rent, that may cause you to fall behind in your mortgage or other expenses. A good property manager will stay on top of your rents and evict those tenants in default if necessary.

Fair Isaac Corporation / FICO score

Named for the score's creators, the FICO score is a type of credit score that makes up a substantial portion of the credit report that lenders use to assess a real estate loan applicant's creditworthiness.

FICO scores reflect the use of five mathematical elements:

1. Payment history

2. Current level of risk or indebtedness

3. Types of credit

4. Length of credit history

5. New credit being requested

A person's FICO score will range between 300 and 850. In general, a FICO score above 650 indicates that the individual has a very good credit history. People with scores below 620 will often find it substantially more difficult to obtain financing at a favorable rate.

Run your credit as soon as you make the decision to invest in real estate. If your FICO is low, a good credit repair company can often help you to clean up your credit quickly and raise your credit score, allowing you to receive a better rate on your loan.

Fiduciary / Fiduciary Duty

When a real estate agent acts in an agency capacity, he or she is legally mandated by duties known as *fiduciary duties*. Fiduciary duties can vary from state to state, but in a broad sense the real estate agent or broker is entrusted with keeping all client information private and confidential and working in the client's best interest at all times.

Fixed-Rate Mortgage

With a fixed-rate mortgage, the interest rate is set when you take out the loan and will not change for the term of the loan. Typically, fixed-rate mortgages are more costly upfront than adjustable-rate mortgages.

Foreclosure

This is the legal process by which a lender may attempt to recover the outstanding balance of a note due when the borrower has failed to make the required mortgage payments. Income-producing properties that fall into foreclosure are rare, but they do occur, and an astute investor oftentimes finds foreclosed properties to be a solid investment. However, beware of these! They can be a real bump in the road. You need to understand how and why the property failed. Remember that someone else purchased this same property and most likely had the same intent; however, they were unsuccessful.

Ask yourself, or better yet, ask your real estate agent a few quick questions:

- Was this failure due to mismanagement?
- Did the previous owner overpay?
- Is there something inherently wrong with this particular property that will cause any investor to fail again?

Remember to move slowly, gather information, and make smart, well-advised moves. Don't jump on it because you have heard foreclosures are good deals. Foreclosures can be complicated transactions, and you will not have much opportunity for due diligence, so make sure you have the right set of eyes on as much information as you can get. Make sure your CPA, financial advisor, wealth manager, and real estate agent are all involved in evaluating the possible purchase.

Gross Rent Multiplier / GRM

The Gross Rent Multiplier, or GRM, is the ratio of the purchase price or assessed value of a property to the property's annual scheduled rents before expenses such as insurance, taxes, etc.

The rate is calculated with a simple formula:

Market Value/Annual Gross Rents = GRM

For example:

$400,000 sale price / $60,000 = 6.67 GRM

Leveraging

Real estate leveraging can be an effective tool for investors to increase their return on investment by growing their portfolio. The key is to avoid making decisions without proper consideration of the areas of risk in leverage. Leveraging allows the borrower to make money on borrowed money. If you have enough equity in your property and you pull some of that equity out to purchase another property, you are in essence borrowing money from yourself to grow your portfolio.

TRAVEL TIP

Leveraging can be a treacherous or lucrative path. Risk can sometimes equal rewards, but be thoughtful.

Lien

A lien is a legal claim against a property and must be paid off when the property is sold. Mortgages, or first-trust deeds, are considered liens. Since property taxes are generally paid in arrears, tax liens are common. Unpaid vendors who have won a judgment against a property owner may have placed a *Mechanics Lien* on the property. All liens must be paid off before title can transfer to a buyer.

Loan Estimate

The loan estimate is designed to provide disclosures that will be helpful to consumers in understanding the key features, costs, and risks of the mortgage loan for which they are applying. The loan estimate must be provided to consumers no later than three business days after they submit the loan application.

Loan Officer / Lender

You may hear the loan officer referred to by a variety of other titles such as loan representative, loan rep, account executive, and lender. The loan officer has various responsibilities and serves several duties. Loan officers not only solicit loans, they represent the lending institution to the borrower, and they represent the borrower to the lending institution.

TRAVEL TIP *Picking the right lender is extremely important. Keep in mind you are not just buying a property, you are also buying a payment. Choose carefully with the long journey in mind.*

Loan Servicing

Once you obtain a loan, the company you make the payments to will be servicing your loan-processing payments, sending statements, and managing the escrow/impound account. In some cases, the loan servicer ensures that insurance and property taxes are paid on the property, handles pay-offs and assumptions, and provides a variety of other services.

Loan-to-Value Percentage

The loan-to-value percentage correlates the amount of the loan and the appraised value or sales price (whichever of the two is lower). The formula looks like this:

$$\text{Loan-to-Value Ratio} = \frac{\text{Mortgage Amount}}{\text{Appraised Property Value}}$$

Mortgage

A mortgage is a legal document that binds a property to the lender as security for payment of a debt. You may also hear a mortgage referred to as a *first* or *second trust deed*.

Mortgage Banker

Mortgage bankers generally originate and fund their own loans, which are then sold on the secondary market, usually to Fannie Mae, Freddie Mac, or Ginnie Mae. Oftentimes, many types of lenders will loosely refer to themselves as mortgage bankers, even those who are simply mortgage brokers.

Mortgage Broker

The mortgage broker originates loans with a variety of other lending institutions with which they usually have pre-established relationships. A mortgage broker does not fund a loan. The advantage of working with a mortgage broker is that, because they typically represent a large array of lenders, they can offer a greater variety of rates and terms from which to choose.

Mortgagee / Mortgagor

In a mortgage agreement, the mortgagee is the lender, and the mortgagor is the borrower.

Net Operating Income / NOI

NOI is a calculation that is used to determine the annual income generated after all potential necessary operating expenses have been deducted. It is a pre-tax amount and excludes principal and interest payments on loans, amortization, and capital expenditures.

Negative Amortization / Neg Am

Be wary of negative amortization loans and to some extent, be wary of a lender who suggests such a loan. Negative amortization loans serve a purpose, but in general my opinion is a neg am loan is typically a bad idea. Here is how they work. Certain adjustable-rate mortgages allow the interest rate to fluctuate independently of a required minimum payment. If a borrower makes the minimum payment, it may not cover all of the interest that would normally be due at the current interest rate. In essence, the borrower is deferring the interest payment. This is called *deferred interest*. The deferred interest is added to the balance of the loan, increasing the loan balance instead of decreasing it, hence the term *negative amortization*.

Non-recourse Loan / Non-recourse Debt

A non-recourse loan is a loan or debt that is secured by collateral, typically real property; however, the borrower is not personally liable.

Notice of Default / NOD

A notice of default is a written notice from a lender to a borrower that a default has occurred and that legal action may be taken. This is typically the first step in a foreclosure; however, most borrowers who receive notices of default do not end up in foreclosure as they understand the gravity of a NOD and act accordingly. In simple English, a NOD says, "Pay the mortgage or else!"

Passive Income / Mailbox Income

Passive income also known commonly as *mailbox income*, refers to money being earned with little or no effort on the part of the person receiving the funds. In real estate, passive income is the net proceeds distributed to the owner or owners after all expenses have been paid.

Percentage Points / Points

Loan points are a charge to the borrower in connection with obtaining a real estate loan. In theory, the more loan points paid up front, the lower the interest will be over the life of the loan. The term *points* is short for percentage points. If you are charged one point, it equates to one percent of the loan amount.

For example:

$300,000 loan at 1 point = 1% of $300,000 or $3,000

Pre-Approval

In general, a pre-approval means that the borrower has completed a loan application and provided debt, income, and savings documentation, which may or may not have been reviewed and approved by an underwriter. A pre-approval is typically done at a certain loan amount and makes assumptions about what the interest rate will actually be at the time the loan is funded. A true pre-approval would also make estimates for the amount including the property taxes, insurance, and other general operating costs. A pre-approval applies only to the borrower. Once a buyer chooses a property, the property must also meet the lender's underwriting guidelines.

Prepayment / Prepay

A prepayment can take many forms. Any time a borrower pays more than the scheduled payment, that payment is considered a prepayment. Payments in full on a mortgage, sale of the property, or a foreclosure are also prepayment occurrences. In each case, prepayment means payment occurs before the loan has been fully amortized.

Prepayment Penalty

A prepayment penalty is a fee that some lending institutions charge a borrower who pays off a loan before it is due. Many loans are subject to pre-payment penalties, and oftentimes the pre-payment penalty is on a sliding scale, typically decreasing over time. Make sure you ask about pre-payment penalties before funding your loan.

Preliminary Title Report / The Prelim

A preliminary title report provides a great deal of pertinent information about the property that is essential for a buyer to see such as how title is currently held and what kind of exceptions to title are currently on record (for example, easements, liens, and encumbrances). The preliminary title report then becomes the final title report on which title insurance is based. In addition to specific exceptions to title that will be listed on a title report, it will also list standard exclusions from coverage.

In virtually every real estate transaction, the buyer reserves the right to approve or object to the preliminary title report and unilaterally cancel the transaction unless the seller can provide a clear title by eliminating certain exceptions prior to closing. However, a buyer will only have a limited time period (typically around 14 to 21 days) during which to act on the review of a title report.

It's extremely important for a buyer to carefully review a title report immediately and to take appropriate action if there are any unacceptable exceptions to title. Title reports can be lengthy and confusing to the novice real estate investor.

Make sure your title officer and real estate agent are a second and third set of eyes on the title report. Know what you are buying before you sign off.

Pre-Qualification / Pre-Qual

A pre-qual is a lender's written opinion of a borrower's ability to qualify for a home loan and is issued after the loan officer has made inquiries about debt, income, and savings.

The information provided to the loan officer may have been presented verbally or in the form of documentation, and the loan officer may or may not have reviewed a credit report on the borrower.

Principal Balance / The Principal

The principal is the amount borrowed or remaining unpaid; it is the part of the monthly payment that reduces the remaining mortgage balance.

Prime Rate / The Prime

The prime rate is the interest rate that banks charge their preferred customers. Typically, these most credit-worthy customers are large corporations.

Pro Forma

Pro forma is the income that you project will be obtained from an investment property by increasing the rents to market value. Oftentimes, a listing will be presented with pro forma numbers rather than actual rents. Ideally, this will be disclosed up front, but always ask the listing agent to verify if the numbers presented are actual. If you do use pro forma numbers to calculate your return, make sure to do a rental survey of the area, and check to see what type of rent restrictions may apply within the city. Review each tenant's lease to determine how viable the pro forma numbers will be.

Promissory Note

This is a legally binding, written promise that specifies the amount to be repaid, the time period, and the terms and conditions.

Qualified Intermediary / The Accommodator

A qualified intermediary sometimes referred to simply as a *QI* acts as a sort of middleman ensuring that the 1031 exchange meets all Internal Revenue Service Code section 1031 tax-deferred exchanges rules and regulations. The qualified intermediary holds the proceeds from the sale of the relinquished property in a trust or escrow account in order to ensure the entity or individual exchanging the property never has actual or constructive receipt of the sale proceeds.

If the seller of the property that is being exchanged takes receipt of the money, the exchange is "blown," and a 1031 cannot be facilitated. Be very careful, know the rules, and set up a qualified intermediary long before closing on your sale.

Qualifying Ratios

These ratios are calculations used for determining whether or not a borrower can qualify for a mortgage.

Quitclaim Deed

A quitclaim deed is a legal instrument by which the owner of a piece of real property, called the *grantor*, transfers any interest to a recipient or *grantee*. The owner/grantor terminates or *quits* any right and claim to the property, allowing the right or claim to transfer to the recipient/grantee.

A quitclaim deed is often mistakenly referred to as a "quick claim deed."

Relinquished Property / The Down Leg

This term refers to the property to be sold or disposed of by the exchangor in a 1031 or tax-deferred, like-kind exchange transaction.

Replacement Property / The Up Leg

Replacement property is the like-kind property acquired or exchanged by the exchangor in a 1031 tax-deferred, like-kind exchange transaction.

Real Estate Owned / REO

An REO is a property that goes back to the mortgage company after an unsuccessful foreclosure auction. Often foreclosure auctions do not result in the successful sale of a foreclosed property. If there had been enough equity in the property to satisfy the loan, the owner would have sold the property and paid off the bank. That is typically why the property ends up at a foreclosure or trustee sale.

Once the bank owns the property, the mortgage loan no longer exists. The bank may evict the owner or tenants, if necessary, and may do some repairs, but don't count on it. Most of these properties are sold as is. The bank may negotiate with the IRS for removal of tax liens and oftentimes will pay off any home-owners' association dues. As a purchaser of an REO property, the buyer will receive a title insurance policy and may have a very limited or no opportunity to investigate the property.

A bank-owned property may or may not be a great bargain. Do your homework before making an offer. Make sure that the price you are offering makes sense for the area, the condition, and the expenses you may encounter to rehab the property. Don't get caught up in a bidding war and pay over market value. REOs are not always a bargain. Oftentimes, buyers make the mistake of not consulting a realtor with an REO and attempting to deal directly with a bank. Don't get lured into the idea of getting a bargain. REOs are very tricky. An astute real estate agent is invaluable when reviewing an REO. Remember, as a buyer you are not paying your real estate agent directly. The seller is. Since their fee is already built in, don't think you will get a better deal without a realtor. Typically, the opposite happens. If you choose to travel this road without your own realtor representation, proceed with caution!

When you consider the costs of an REO renovation, including carry costs (mortgage, taxes, insurance, utilities, maintenance) until completion, this can be an expensive journey.

Return On Investment / ROI

The ROI is a performance measure used to evaluate and compare the productivity of income-producing properties. ROI measures the gain or the loss on an investment property relative to the dollar amount invested. There are different ways to calculate ROI, but in general the formula looks like this:

ROI = (Net Profit / Cost of Investment) x 100

A property with a poor ROI may still represent a great opportunity. Many properties have rents well under market or are poorly managed. If you can see a way to turn the ROI around, you may have found a diamond in the rough.

Short Sale

A short sale is a sale of real estate in which the proceeds from the sale are insufficient to cover the balance of the amount owed on the outstanding liens. Remember that a short sale is a privilege and not a right. A property and the mortgagee must qualify by the lenders' standards to have a short sale approved. The bank will consider its best interests before approving a short sale or moving forward with foreclosure.

Straight-Line Depreciation

Straight-line depreciation refers to the method of calculating amortization (depreciation) by dividing the difference between a property's cost and its expected salvage value by the number of years it is expected to be useful.

Tax Deferred Exchange / 1031 Exchange / 1031

Simply stated, a 1031 tax exchange allows the seller of a property to defer paying the taxable portion of the sale proceeds of an income-producing property by trading or replacing the property for another like-kind property of equal or greater value. To qualify as a 1031 exchange, the transaction must take the form of an exchange rather than just a sale of one property with the subsequent purchase of another. First, to be like kind, the property being sold and the new replacement property must both be held for investment purposes (your primary residence will not qualify); however, the properties do not need to be of an exact similar type. For example, you could trade a mountain cabin you used as a rental property for an office building that you will be renting to tenants. The logistics and process of selling a property and then buying another property are practically identical to any typical property sale except for the time frames and 1031 rules.

A 1031 exchange is unique because the entire transaction is treated as an exchange and not just as a straight sale. This difference allows the taxpayer to qualify for a deferrerence of taxable gains under IRS guidelines. Make sure you are using a qualified 1031 intermediary (also known as an *accommodator*) for the exchange, and consult with them on all the rules before entering into the exchange process. There is also a reverse 1031 exchange, which is a tax-deferment strategy when (for a range of reasons) the replacement property must be purchased before the relinquished or exchanged property is sold. It is more complex and more costly than a typical 1031 exchange and requires careful planning.

TRAVEL TIP

A 1031 tax exchange does not alleviate your tax burden; it simply delays payment of the taxes until the exchanged property is sold.

The 1031 exchange rules and time frames require that:

- *Properties must be "like kind."*
- *They mush be of equal or greater value and equal or greater debt.*
- *You must identify a replacement property within 45 calendar days.*
- *The exchange must be executed within 180 calendar days (runs concurrently with the 45 days to identify).*
- *You utilize and consult with an exchange accommodator.*

Title Insurance / Title Policy

Title insurance protects the purchaser and the mortgage holder against financial loss due to title and lien problems. The title insurance policy is meant to protect both a purchaser's and a financial institution's interests in real property. There are different types of title insurance available. Seek the advice of your title representative as to which policy best suits your needs with each individual property. All properties are not created equal; the same is true for title policies. Make sure you find the one that is right for your investment. Title insurance policies can differ from state to state. As an example, in California there is both a CLTA (California Land Title Association Policy) and an ALTA (American Land Title Association Policy) that cover the following:

CLTA policy will protect you against the most basic issues associated with your home's title and against anything maintained in public records such as easements, recorded liens or other encumbrances.

ALTA policy provides the same coverage as a CLTA policy as well as additional coverage for unrecorded defects in the title. A survey of the property may be conducted by the title insurance company prior to issuance of an ALTA policy, since it may ensure against unrecorded encroachments and easements involving the boundary lines.

Umbrella Insurance Policy / Umbrella Policy

Umbrella policies are well named. They are intended to be extra liability insurance coverage supplementing your basic liability policy, typically covering multiple properties.

Underwriting / Underwriters

Underwriting refers to the process that a bank or other lending institution uses to evaluate a customer's eligibility when qualifying for a loan. The perceived value of the property to be purchased will also be evaluated.

When real estate agents and clients refer to underwriting, they often look as if they have bitten into a lemon. However, you should appreciate the underwriting process. The underwriters are the guardians of the lending industry. It is their job to make sure that potential buyers have represented themselves and their finances in an accurate way. Their standards are much higher than loan pre-qualification requirements, which are just a starting point and give an overview of what loan dollar amount the lender believes the buyer will qualify for. The actual underwriting process includes in-depth reviews of several factors, which can include tax returns, debt-to-income ratio, recent sales of comparable properties, personal credit scores, and the property's income and expense records.

Value Add

The term *value add* is used to refer to properties that are seen as quick money-making opportunities. Typically, these are properties that require improvements that will increase their value and or cash flow. The improvements can range from minor to full remodels.

Value-add investments require an understanding of what consumers are looking for and an ability to determine accurate costs and time frames in which the project can be completed. Factoring the actual dollars you will spend versus the return you anticipate is essential before making an offer on a value-add property.

Worker's Compensation Insurance / Worker's Comp

Worker's compensation is a form of insurance that covers an employee who is hurt on the job. These policies most often have a clause that includes wage replacement and medical benefits in exchange for mandatory relinquishment of the employee's right to sue his or her employer. As the property owner, you want to ensure that your vendors or anyone you employ directly has purchased their own worker's compensation insurance to lessen your exposure to a lawsuit should a vendor be injured on the job.

Write-Off

The IRS tends to favor real estate investors, providing more tax benefits than most any other investment. Here are a few main deductions:

- Interest paid on your loan
- Depreciation of the property
- Repairs to the property
- Business-related travel
- Property insurance
- Home office if you are running your business from there
- Wages to independent contractors

Perpetuity

I saved the best definition for last. Websters online dictionary defines *Perpetuity* as: "An annuity payable forever."

My goal in writing this book is to guide you to an everlasting stream of income — an income in *Perpetuity*.

Tales from the Road

Travelogue #2
Avoiding the Toll Roads

I once had a client, named David, who came to me shortly after his wife had passed away. David explained to me that he and his wife Helen had discussed downsizing, but the thought of moving out of the house they had raised their family in made for melancholy feelings, so the decision to move was continually shelved. After Helen passed away, David's perspective on the house changed dramatically. The house had become a sad reminder of a loving partner and a life gone by. David was finally ready to move. David and Helen had owned their home for over 20 years, and they had seen strong market appreciation over those two decades. David wanted to downsize from four to two bedrooms. He also wanted to be on a single level as the stairs in his current home were wreaking havoc with his knees. Most importantly, he wanted a view of the ocean and to be geographically closer his daughter.

David contacted me about selling, and he was pleased when I told him the value of his current home, but he was shocked when I told him what the average list price was for a condo fitting his search criteria. I suggested David speak with both his financial advisor and his accountant before making the decision to sell. A day later, David called me back with the sad news that he simply could not afford to move. I asked what the issues were. David's financial advisor had told him that the purchase of a new home would greatly increase his property taxes and in turn make his cash flow far too tight.

I asked David if he had spoken to his tax advisor. He had not. I suggested that he contact his CPA and discuss Proposition 60, which allows a California homeowner over the age of 55 to transfer their tax basis with them a single time if they purchase a primary residence for equal or lesser value (there are, of course, other restrictions and rules, but that is the basic take). Two days later, David called me back with the mixed news that although Proposition 60 would help to greatly reduce the monthly cost of his desired new condo, his accountant felt the association dues were too high for David to take on with his fixed income. Again, David was distraught. He truly wanted his ocean view condo near his daughter. Now I was distraught, too. I could hear the sad disappointment in his voice. David's lack of cash flow was stopping him from living out his golden years in his dream home closer to his family. Money was the issue, but in this case, money was also the answer.

I reminded David that the first $250,000 in proceeds from the sale of his house would be tax-free. I suggested that David buy his dream home and an income-producing property; the proceeds of which would offset the cost of the high HOA dues on the condo. He liked the idea, and after a little more research, he called me back and excitedly said, "Let's do it!"

I listed David's house and quickly found three qualified buyers. Next up was the income property search. I located a two-bedroom condo in a college town that had great rental history. David used his $250,0000 of tax-free gains from the sale of his home to purchase the condo. The rents from the investment property easily paid for the expense of the rental property with enough left over to cover the expense of the condo's HOA dues plus a little extra to put in his pocket every month. The cash flow off the condo and the anticipated annual appreciation of the property far outweighed the ultra-conservative bonds David's financial advisor had originally suggested he invest in. David got his dream condo and cash flow in *Perpetuity*.

Rules of the Road

Rule # 2

Good deals are not found;
they are crafted.

Now, one thing I tell everyone is, learn about real estate. Repeat after me: real estate provides the highest returns, the greatest values and the least risk.

Armstrong Williams

Chapter 3
Choosing Your Travel Partners

"In business for yourself, not by yourself."
– Ray Kroc

I cannot stress enough the importance of selecting the right team members to accompany you on this endeavor. Your team can be the wind in your sails, speeding you on your way, or the broken spike that will derail your entire journey. My best advice is, don't try to do this alone. Being your own real estate agent or property inspector is not a good idea. The amount you will pay for quality service can potentially save you thousands of dollars before and after you acquire the property.

There are a few key questions you need to ask each member of your travel team. Use the worksheet on pages 111-114 to track your interviews. You can also download free, PDF forms at www.DestinationPerpetuity.com.

Arguably the most valuable member of your buyers' team is also the one that costs you nothing. So let's start there.

The Real Estate Agent / Your New BFF

If you're a first-time buyer, you may not know that you do not directly pay your agent as a buyer; the seller does. In almost every transaction, the agent's commissions are predetermined as a percentage of the sale price at the time the listing agent and the seller sign a listing contract. Both the commission paid to the seller's agent and the buyer's agent (sometimes different percentages) are deducted from the sale proceeds.

Your agent may ask you to sign an agency disclosure. This acknowledges that your agent has a fiduciary duty to you and your real estate transaction. Your agent's job is to locate the right property, negotiate a sales price with your instruction, and follow the sales process through until the transaction has closed.

Your real estate agent will oversee the other aspects of the transaction such as title, escrow, physical inspection, loan process, etc. That is not to say your agent is in charge of these processes or the individuals that provide these services within the transaction; actually, the contrary is true. Your agent should not be giving you advice on matters outside of what he/she is licensed to do. Your agent should, however, have a working knowledge of these matters and watch for red flags in the transaction. Remember, each team member has a specific task he/she performs. Your real estate agent can help you select and to some degree oversee the other members of your travel team.

A good agent can and should verify on an ongoing basis that each member of the team is completing his or her portion of the transaction in a professional and timely manner. Think of your real estate agent as the driver of the transaction, keeping your journey on course for a successful and timely closing.

So, let's consider what makes an agent a good choice and what type of agent you should perhaps avoid. Let's start with the latter.

As on any journey, you want to steer clear of potholes that might make for a rocky ride. We are looking for a smooth journey with a safe, secure arrival. Oftentimes, when buyers find a property they like, they go directly to the listing agent and ask him/her to represent them. Many buyers do this thinking they will get a better deal by getting the inside scoop on the property. Actually the opposite is more commonly true.

Why? The answer is simple; the listing agent has signed a contract with the seller and in doing so, he or she has accepted a fiduciary duty to act in the seller's best interest. The selling agent has been tasked with getting the highest price possible with the best terms for the seller. How then can the same agent also perform a fiduciary duty for you as the buyer? Remember, when you sign an agency agreement with a buyer's agent, he or she accepts a fiduciary duty to you and that duty is to then get you, the buyer, the most favorable price and terms. The two objectives seem at odds. So how can this be accomplished?

There are times when a skilled and ethical agent can successfully represent both sides and carve out a fair deal, but that requires a reputable agent who understands the nuances and responsibilities of representing both sides of a transaction. This is commonly known as *dual agency*. In such cases, a single agent who understands and appreciates the importance of his or her fiduciary responsibility can even be an asset, leading both parties towards a fair and equitable agreement. But if you don't know the agent, beware. You may or may not have an agent that is looking out for both the buyer's and seller's best interests, or you may have an agent who is just looking at a double commission. Don't think that by going directly to the listing agent you will be getting a better deal. Even the most trustworthy agent will have some level of conflict with representing both parties. If you have any doubts about the listing agent and his or her ability to represent your best interests in a dual-agency transaction, you should consider bringing in your own representation. Since the total commission for both buyer and seller agents was determined when the listing was signed, having your own agent will cost you no additional fees. Remember, the seller pays the commissions. The seller and listing agent have already entered into an agency agreement binding the listing agent with the fiduciary responsibility to the seller. So who do you want representing you as the buyer?

Selecting the right real estate agent is extremely important. Take your time, and do your homework. This choice can greatly influence the success or failure of your journey.

Her postcard says she's #1 in the area. She must be the best!

Be careful with the #1 agent in the area. You might be tempted to call an agent who has pages of ads for sale every week. An agent claiming to be the #1 agent is most likely a

WORLD'S GREATEST REALTOR
#1
Pick me, your area expert!

very successful agent and probably knows the business inside and out. So why is that agent not necessarily a good choice? The answer is time.

When you are a buyer selecting a property to purchase, the process can be extremely time consuming for your real estate agent. A good agent may spend hundreds of hours searching and previewing properties solely on your behalf before showing you a handful to discuss. The #1 agent is typically far too busy servicing their listings to spend that much time on an individual buyer, and all too often, buyers working with this level agent will be handed off to a team member who acts as a buyer's agent for the busy superstar. Oftentimes, these buyer's agents are highly skilled and you may well be in good hands, but have a discussion about who will be working with you, and involve yourself in selecting the buyer's agent that you feel comfortable with. Don't be fooled into thinking that the #1 agent is the best choice simply because of a momentary sales status sent on a random postcard.

Also, be careful not to choose an agent simply because they are a family member or a friend. Purchasing income property is far different than selecting a home to purchase. Real estate agents who represent income-producing properties must have an advanced skill set. They must understand what determines a gross multiplier, how to calculate a cap rate, and a multitude of other specific bits of knowledge.

Your cousin may have his or her real estate license, but be careful. The choice of your real estate agent is one of the most important selections you will make in building your team. Choosing a real estate agent to avoid hurt feelings or keep goodwill in the family is a bad idea. Friendships and family harmony will really be damaged if you are steered to the wrong purchase and end up with a property that costs you cash as opposed to making you money.

Remember, this is a business transaction and quite possibly the most important one that you will make in your lifetime. This is about your financial freedom. Don't worry about being uncomfortable at Thanksgiving dinner because you did not choose your sister-in-law. What you need to be concerned about is *lifetime* cash flow. Choose your agent based on experience, references, and qualifications as opposed to blood, marriage or friendship.

Make sure you select a real estate agent that is a member of the National Association of Realtors® (www.realtor.org). Also, make sure your agent belongs to a local board of realtors. These real estate agents, known as Realtors®, adhere to the highest standards of ethics and service.

So now that we know you are most likely not going to choose the listing agent, the #1 area agent, or your crazy uncle, where do you start? Referrals!

Begin by asking someone you know who owns income-producing properties what real estate agent he or she recommends. The more referrals you get, the better. Inquire around. Speak with everyone you know who owns income-producing real estate, ask them the following questions, and take notes:

Are you happy with the investment?

_____

_____

_____

_____

_____

Were you happy with your realtor?

_____

_____

_____

_____

_____

Is the property performing as anticipated?

_____

_____

_____

_____

_____

Are you thinking about buying another income-producing property?

This question might seem nosy, but it's actually important in helping you decide if this person's agent is right for you. Most anyone who purchases the right property will want to purchase more.

Would you use the same agent again?

Pay close attention to how this question is answered. If you sense hesitation with an endorsement, this may not be a good choice for you. Remember, this is possibly the biggest and most important investment you will make in your life. Take your time to find an agent for whom past clients will cheerlead. If an agent did their job well, past clients will sing their praises loudly and without hesitation.

If you receive enthusiastically positive remarks, your next question is simple: What's your agent's phone number?

(   ) __ __ __ - __ __ __ __

So, what if you don't know anyone who has purchased an apartment building? No problem. Your local real estate office can help. But like everything else along our journey, there are rules to the road, so be careful here. Don't just walk in and ask to speak to an agent. Most brokerages have what is called *floor time*, and the *floor agents* are typically well qualified for most types of residential real estate transactions. Income-producing properties, however, are a niche specialty, and few agents truly understand this submarket. Instead of just walking in, make an appointment to meet with the branch manager. The branch manager will know with whom to place you right away, but ask to speak with at least two agents, and repeat this exercise with at least two different brokerages. Remember that all real estate agents are independent contractors; although they may work for the same brokerage, they are both competing for your business. When you interview them, let them know you are speaking to a *few agents*. Also, let the branch manager know you will be interviewing agents at a competing office. The branch manager will want to keep the business in his or her own office and will want to make sure you are being matched with the right sales associate.

Once you have selected the agents to interview, you will want to ask some initial key questions. This will help you weed through any agents that are potentially the wrong choice. Get your pen ready; you are about to take more notes.

How much of your business comes from the sale of income-producing properties?

The answer you want to hear is 100 percent, but as little as 25 percent can be an acceptable answer.

Do you have any referrals from past clients?

It is great if they do; however, if they don't, it doesn't mean they shouldn't be considered.

Do you personally own any income property?

Again, it is not a deal breaker if the agent does not own apartment buildings, but it is a big plus if they do. Being an investor gives an agent a higher level of understanding as to the nuances and process of selecting the right property.

Will I be working directly with you or with a buyer's agent?

As I discussed earlier, many top agents use a team of buyer's agents, which is fine; however, you will want to interview the team member you will be working with and ask the same questions of that agent.

Here is a fun and very telling question:

Can you explain to me the difference between a cap rate and a gross multiplier?

As I discussed in *Chapter 2: Learning the Language*, these are basic terms and formulas, and any real estate agent that truly specializes in income-producing properties will not shy away from answering your questions in detail. If the agent fails to give good, clear answers, you should really think twice before selecting him/her.

What do you think is the most important quality of an income-producing property?

There is no right or wrong answer here, but it is an interesting question that may reveal if this agent is a good fit for your goals. Perhaps he/she sees future appreciation as the most important consideration while you are looking for cash flow. I believe differing opinions can lead to positive conversations and help weed through the wrong properties. Many factors need to be considered and multiple viewpoints should be welcomed. For the most part, you should select an agent of like mind. If you share a common vision with your agent, you will find a smoother journey through the process and most likely greater satisfaction in the end result.

Now that you have your real estate agent in the driver's seat, you might think it's time to hit the road and go shopping. Not so fast. We have more seats to fill before we fire up the engine. Unless you are paying cash for your property, you will need a lender. The lender is a key travel partner. Unless you have a rich and generous uncle, keep this companion close by and in constant contact. Your lender is very important to the journey; keep him or her on speed dial.

The Lender

The process of locating a lender is similar to the process in which you found your real estate agent. Asking for referrals. The same person who recommended your real estate agent most likely

used a lender. Your real estate agent will also have a lender of choice, if not several. Interview at least three lenders. Lenders are not all alike; they can be bank loan officers, mortgage brokers, or direct lenders/mortgage lenders:

- **Bank Loan Officer** — This person typically works for a lending institution. Bank lending policies typically are very conservative and therefore, offer fewer options that may limit your choices. That is not to say they will not have the best loan, but shopping around is highly recommended.

- **Mortgage Broker** — A mortgage broker is an individually licensed person or firm that finds loans for investors considering purchasing property. They may work with banks, credit unions, trust companies, mortgage corporations, or any number of financial companies. A mortgage broker is a middleman of sorts between the buyer and the lending institution. Typically, a mortgage broker will have far more programs for a consumer than a direct lender or bank.

- **Direct Lender/Mortgage Lender** — This is a licensed person or firm that originates the loan and oversees the processes of underwriting, funding, and closing. Most direct lenders have access to a wide variety of loans for the consumer. Oftentimes, one of these options includes funding with the lender's own money.

The Property Inspector

The property inspector will be a very important member of your crew. A good property inspector can spot hidden issues that the seller may or may not be aware of. Regardless of prior knowledge, once the problem is brought to light, the repair or cost of repair becomes an issue and may or may not be negotiated into the transaction. If a serious issue is brought to the buyer's attention during the due-diligence process, the buyer's agent can attempt to negotiate a resolution to the issue prior to close of the transaction. Sometimes the deal can even be *re-traded*, meaning that a renegotiation of the sale price takes place based on a previously unknown or undisclosed issue of a major repair. Here's an example. Let's say that your property inspector detects that the older hot tub in the back yard of the duplex you are buying is inoperable and missing a number of parts. This is the same hot tub that was featured in the property listing as an *amenity*. In this case, you might either renegotiate the sale price for the repair value of the hot tub or get an allowance for having to pay someone to haul it off the property. Re-trading the deal is a difficult process and one that often ends a transaction; but in certain situations, an astute real estate agent can use such information as an effective negotiation tactic.

A really good inspector will find most every issue with the property and bring it to your attention. Oftentimes, the buyer will not want the property after learning about a serious problem with its physical condition. Hence the nickname, *deal killers*. Don't get me wrong; if the property has a cracked foundation, then that is information you need to know.

However, oftentimes these reports will call out minor issues as needing, "...further inspection by a licensed professional" — standard boilerplate language added as liability protection for the home inspection company. The wording of these disclaimers can seem ominous. A reputable home inspector will advise you of what is and what is not an issue of true concern. Don't get spooked by the report. Follow the advice given, and get a licensed professional in the appropriate field to give you a more in-depth analysis of any issues brought to your attention that are beyond the scope of the inspector.

The Insurance Agent

Your lender will require a policy covering fire and other potential liabilities. Even if you are paying cash and do not have a lender involved, you should always carry sufficient liability insurance to cover your investment. When you interview insurance agents, ask about various types of coverage. Not all insurance policies are the same, and not all insurance companies offer similar coverage. You may also want to discuss insurance policies that are not required by the lender such as content, earthquake, and water damage insurance. They can be expensive, but *Mother Nature* can do some real damage. Depending on where your property is located, extra insurance might be a good bet. Be prepared.

TRAVEL
TIP

If you own multiple properties, you should consider discussing the various pros and cons of an additional "umbrella policy" with your agent. My short answer is that more insurance is a good thing.

Certified Public Accountant / CPA

If you are going to own property, a certified public accountant (CPA) will be an important and invaluable travel companion. Your CPA should be consulted prior to making any major financial decisions. Remember, this is the person who will be filing your  taxes and acting as your pipeline with the IRS. A good CPA can save you tons of money. A bad one? Let's not even go there, other than to say that an accountant who is not a CPA should not be considered. Time to get more referrals. Your real estate agent will be an excellent place to start. Most agents who sell income-producing real estate typically own some themselves. They most likely have already done the vetting for you and will have the name of a qualified CPA. With that said, it is still wise to interview two or three. Ideally, you want to choose a CPA for the long run. Make sure you select not only someone who was highly recommended, but also someone that you like, trust, and feel comfortable working with. You will be talking to them a lot.

Certified Financial Planner / CFP

A good CFP can help with planning and decision making for all kinds of investments. Most certified financial planners see the value of a truly diversified investment portfolio, which includes real estate — an easy point to argue when you understand the majority of the world's wealth is held in real estate. Financial advisors who only push you toward stocks, bonds, and mutual funds may be thinking more about their commissions than your long-term retirement goals. If real estate is not part of your financial planner's program, perhaps you should consider a new financial planner. Most financial planners I have spoken with like to see 25 to 40 percent of a portfolio in real estate investment. I would argue for a higher percentage, but the bottom line is that real estate is a stable base that should comprise a sizeable percentage of any investment portfolio. Get at least three references, and make sure you feel comfortable with your pick.

Title Agent / Title Officer / Title Rep

As with many of the other travel companions, not all title insurance representatives are created equal. Make certain you have a title insurance agent that is actually reviewing the title and not just issuing a policy. Most real estate brokerages have an affiliated title company, and typically those title officers associated with an established office have earned their way there.

Reviewing the title report is extremely important. It's a dry read that has to be done. All eyes should be on it. Yours, the real estate agent's, the lender's, and most importantly, the title officer's. A good title officer should review the entire title.

Property Management Company

Start thinking about whether or not you want to manage your property yourself or hire a professional management team. There are pros and cons to both. In a nutshell, it's all about time and money. It will cost you time to manage your own property, and it will cost you money to have someone else manage it for you.

You have three important choices to consider:

1. Hire a professional property manager to take care of everything.
2. Co-manage the property with a management company.
3. Be your own property manager.

If you hire a professional property management company, there are local and national companies that will oversee every aspect of your investment property including vacancy, maintenance, landscaping, bookkeeping, and more. The price you pay for the service depends on the company you hire and the level of service provided. Some state and local laws actually require on-site property management depending on the size and or occupancy of the building. Typically, you should expect to pay a fee of between 5 to 12 percent of the gross rents to a property management company. The percentage you pay will vary depending on the level of service and reputation of the management company. The top professional management company will have a certified property manager (CPM) overseeing the operations. This certification is an important designation. The lack of a CPM designation does not necessarily mean a property management company is unqualified, but having the designation may ensure a higher level of property management skills. Remember the old adage, "You get what you pay for." When it comes to managing your investment, you want to have the best in the business. Paying for the right property manager can make you money. I don't recommend that you try tackling your first building on your own. Delays in filling vacancies and unattended maintenance issues can cost you dearly.

Giving carte blanche to a management company for expenses is never a good idea. Set a reasonable dollar amount that allows the management company to spend monthly at their discretion. This will ensure that you don't get a phone call every time a toilet overflows, but it will also mean that you don't get a surprise bill for a new roof.

I am a big believer in co-managing your own properties with your property manager. No matter how good a property manager is, it will always be in your best interest to keep a hand in the management of your investment. I recommend that you work in tandem with the property management company. Decisions can be made together and situations can be discussed before taking action. You will learn a lot about the business, and the property manager will have to be on his or her toes at all times with you involved. Even if you eventually want to save money and manage your buildings yourself, it's good to start off watching the pros at work. Be a part of every decision, and be present when leases are signed and when major repairs are completed whenever possible.

When you understand the ins and outs of management, you will be better equipped should you ever decide to take over your property. Doing so can save thousands of dollars annually, greatly increasing your cash flow. Just be ready before you take on the task of self-managing; depending on the size and condition of your property, self-management can be extremely time consuming.

If you choose to go it on your own for property management, you will need to assemble a team. Get on the referral train again, and start asking about a good gardener, plumber, electrician, carpenter, etc. Becoming your own property manager can really begin to drive your profits upward. However, if you're just starting out, you might consider a property management company for at least the first year. A great resource for property management referrals is The Apartment Owners Association (www.aoausa.com). There are many regional and local associations that can be found with a simple Web search.

If you choose to work as your own property manager, make certain you have at least two reliable vendors for each category: two electricians, two plumbers, two painters, etc. This will ensure that you always have a backup in case one leaves the business or is unavailable. Let the vendors know each time you offer a job that you are just getting a bid from them. If your vendors know they have competition, they will keep their prices more competitive. Only work with individuals or companies that are licensed, bonded, and insured, and make sure they know their work must always be top notch to ensure that you keep them on your *vendor bid list*. You can save money working with unlicensed vendors, but be careful here. A vendor without a license leaves you little recourse should the job go bad.

Tales from the Road

Travelogue #3
Jill – The Lone Wolf

Jill was an entrepreneur, and after having built and sold two successful businesses, she decided it was time to tackle real estate investments. She got her real estate license and aced the test the first time through. Jill planned to buy a property and be her own agent; thereby earning the commission herself and recouping part of the out-of-pocket money she would need for the down payment. Jill liked the south side of town, and she knew it was a desirable rental area since it was near both a hospital and a college. Jill found what seemed to be a great building — five single units all in seemingly good condition. Jill negotiated with the listing agent and was pleased to get the property for 10 percent less than the asking price. Jill's father was a retired contractor, so Jill decided to ask him to inspect the property. He had built over 40 homes and had been excellent at his job. Jill's father made a list of some minor repairs, and Jill negotiated with the seller's agent to repair nearly the entire list of items her father had called out.

Jill had been remiss in not getting pre-qualified before presenting an offer. She then got busy and contacted her bank and a few other lending institutions that had been recommended by friends and most of the quotes were fairly consistent on the rate, term, and cost of the loan. Then, Jill heard a radio advertisement for an online lending company that advertised an unbelievably low rate. Jill called, and in minutes she was convinced this was the correct route. Vince, the representative for the online company, quoted her an amazing rate with almost no out-of-pocket costs. Jill reviewed her notes and then re-contacted all of the lending institutions she had spoken with to see if they could beat or even match Vince's deal. None could come close. Jill filled out the online application and had Vince begin to process her loan. Being a diligent real estate agent, Jill went about removing her contingencies one by one. However, she ran into her first snag when the appraisal did not come back from the lender on time. Her appraisal and loan contingency periods were nearly up. Jill requested an extension, explaining to the listing agent that the appraisal process was taking longer than expected. The listing agent explained to Jill that the owner was doing an IRS 1031 exchange and was already in escrow on his next property. The agent further explained that there was a backup offer in place for all cash and that this other buyer was now more desirable than Jill to the seller since the all-cash offer could close almost immediately. Jill was issued a *notice to perform*, which stated that as per the purchase agreement, she would need to remove all of her contingencies within 48 hours or she would be in breach of contract, potentially giving the seller the unilateral right to cancel the transaction and go with the other buyer.

Jill called her Internet lender and was told that Vince was no longer with the company. She asked who was handling his files and found out his clients had been divided up among several different online agents at the company. Jill's file could not be immediately located, but Mr. Nelson, Vince's supervisor, assured her he would personally get back to her within 24 hours. After two days went by, Jill called and was told Mr. Nelson had left on vacation and would not be returning for 10 days. Her sale was scheduled to close in less than three weeks. Another supervisor got involved two days later, and her file was located in underwriting. When Jill asked who was covering for Mr. Nelson while he was gone, she was told, "Oh, you can just talk to any of us." Each time Jill called, she got a different representative, and the answer was always the same, "Your file is still being reviewed in underwriting, give it a day or two."

Knowing that there was another anxious buyer waiting in the wings, Jill did not want to let this property get away. She decided to make a business decision. She removed her contingencies in order to honor the contract and move the transaction forward. The next day, Jill heard back from the online lender. The property on which she had a contract for $592,000 only appraised for $510,000.

Jill also found out that since the building had five units, she would need a commercial loan, and the rates for commercial loans were higher than the loan rates originally quoted to her over the phone during her initial call. If Jill tried to cancel the escrow, the seller could sue her for damages, and she could potentially lose her 3 percent deposit. Jill decided to continue with the transaction and had to come up with additional funds to make up the difference. Between borrowing from her 401K and her parents, Jill was able to raise enough money to close the transaction.

Shortly after taking ownership of the building, one of Jill's tenants gave notice. During the walk through of the unit, Jill noticed the refrigerator and stove were gone. The tenant informed Jill that she owned those items and had the right to take them with her. The owner had not informed Jill that most of the tenants owned their own appliances. Had Jill requested estoppels, she would have learned this fact before moving forward. She would have also learned that each tenant had paid two months security deposit plus last month's rent. The seller had not informed Jill about that either, and Jill had not reviewed the leases properly. These oversights cost Jill thousands of dollars, but it was peanuts compared to the tens of thousands of dollars it cost Jill to replace the cracked foundation her contractor / inspector / father had not detected during his inspection of the property. Had Jill properly studied the rental history of the property, she would have noticed a high turnover rate and high-vacancy factor. Had Jill understood the type of building she was buying and the area she was buying in, she would have factored these issues into her offer. If Jill had known how to correctly evaluate a property based on the historical data of the recent comparable sales, she would have never made such a high offer in the beginning or possibly never made an offer at all on what she once thought to be an *amazing deal*.

The good news is that eventually Jill sold the property and broke even. She reinvested her equity back into real estate. When Jill next purchased, she hired an experienced local agent with extensive market knowledge. He introduced her to a qualified lender, a well-trained property inspector, and an exceptional management company. Jill has stuck with her team ever since. She is now the proud owner of three apartment buildings and is currently in the market for her next property.

Rules of the Road

Rule #3

Teamwork works. Don't go at it alone.

Landlords grow rich in their sleep
without working, risking
or economizing

John Start Mill

Chapter 4
Mapping Out Your Journey

"Risk comes from not knowing what you're doing."
– Warren Buffet

Okay, let's face it. No one really likes paperwork, but it's a necessary evil in almost every business. Unless you are 20 years old, you would never just jump on a plane and go somewhere without a hotel reservation and some idea of a travel agenda. Since this journey takes you through the rest of your life, just commit right now to doing a little planning and paperwork. I assure you, that commitment will make for a much smoother journey.

This is the homework chapter. I know, I know; you hate homework. But this assignment is going to help you to feather a fat retirement nest, so don't complain, and pay attention.

In chapter three, I discussed the virtues of choosing the appropriate travel partners. As you interview your real estate agent, your lender, your property inspector, your contractor, and any other travel partners you feel are essential to the journey, you will want to ask the right questions and take lots of notes.

The following pages act as a workbook and feature a series of questions to ask each individual travel partner. Take lots of notes. This is important stuff, and you want to make intelligent and informed decisions. Don't sign on with the first agent or lender you like. People in sales are all generally likable people; liking them is an important element of your selection, but it should not be the sole criteria or even at the top of your list. Statistics show that a very high percentage of buyers and sellers work with the first real estate agent they speak with. Don't be a statistic; be practical, thoughtful, and informed. Be smart.

The following pages feature key questions and workbook space for you to record your answers. It is vital that you take the time to do this simple assignment. Your future depends on it.

If you need additional forms, visit:
www.DestinationPerpetuity.com

Real Estate Agent Profiles:

Agent name:

Referred by:

Additional references:

Are you a member of a local board of realtors?

Number of income properties sold:

Do you use buyer's agents?

Who will be following the details of my transaction?

Do you own income property?

Can you explain the difference between a gross multiplier and a cap rate:

Why should I pick you as my agent?

Do you have references?

Trulia score and comments:

Zillow score and comments:

Notes:

Lender name:

Referred by:

Additional references:

Number of multi-family unit loans funded annually:

Do you have assistants?

Are you available nights and weekends to answer questions?

What do you offer that other lenders do not?

How many lending / financial institutions do you have access to?

Why should I pick you as my lender?

YELP score and comments:

Notes:

Property Inspector Profiles:

Physical inspector name:

Referred by:

Additional references:

Number of multi-family units inspected annually:

What was your experience in the industry prior to home inspection?

Are you a member of the National Association of Home Inspectors (NAHI) or a state or local home inspectors association?

Will you come back to re-inspect after repairs?

Do you have workmen's comp insurance?

YELP score and comments:

Notes:

Property Management Profiles:

Management company:

Referred by:

Additional references:

Number of multi-family units currently being managed:

Are you and your company licensed as a property management firm by the state?

Are you a member of the Better Business Bureau?

What do you charge for your service?

Do you have workmen's comp insurance?

YELP score and comments:

Notes:

Now, if you are thinking about self-managing, let's get the next list going as well.

Upkeep and repairs are essential to maintaining the value of your property and maximizing your rents. If you are planning to manage your own building, you will want to go back to all your fellow apartment building owners with whom you originally consulted about real estate agent and lender referrals and hit them up again for individual maintenance vendor references. I suggest you do this even if your management company has their own crew.

Once you own an income-producing property, your cash flow depends in great part on your level of involvement in maintaining your property. Whether you use a property management company or self manage your property, do yourself a favor — have options available so that when you get a bid on a roof repair that seems excessive, you will have at least two other roofers to give you competitive bids. If you create this list now and update it as you go, it will be invaluable. Trust me, this list can save you a lot of money with only a little effort on your part.

Start researching maintenance people before you need them, and keep a list of backups. Make sure all your vendors are licensed, bonded, and insured. Some vendors, such as a handyman and a gardener, may not have a formal license, but make sure that they at least carry worker's compensation insurance. Ideally, you should have at least two solid, local references for each of the roles described on pages 116 and 117.

- **Painters** — The elements can wreak havoc on the exterior of your property, and tenants can do similar damage inside. Curb appeal on the outside and light and bright on the inside help to keep units fully occupied.

- **Plumbers** — A large percentage of maintenance issues will have to do with water. Get a good, honest plumber. Referrals and testimonials are extremely important in your search. These guys can make or break your maintenance budget.

- **Electricians** — Electrical issues can cost you big time and pose a huge liability. Mitigate your problems before they happen by making sure the electrical system is up to date and up to code. The last thing you want is a fire due to a faulty electrical system.

- **General Handyman** — This may be your most frequently used phone number. A good handyman can often handle smaller jobs that a full-time plumber or electrician would charge you a great deal more for.

- **Cleaning Crew** — Oftentimes, a good cleaning crew is all you need to get a unit ready to rent. Even if the unit requires a more extensive makeover, a cleaning crew will still be needed for windowsills, toilets, and all the little jobs.

- **Carpet Cleaning Service** — Replacing carpet is expensive. I highly recommend hardwood floors, but if you buy carpet, spend a little extra and get a quality carpet. If you have it cleaned regularly, it can last for years, and you can often avoid re-carpeting each time a unit turns over.

- **Roofers** — Roofs have a life span. Depending on the type of roof and the climate you are in, roofs can last 25 years or more, but only if maintained properly. Once you own your building, you will want to have the roof inspected periodically. A good roofer can typically extend the estimated life span with ongoing maintenance.

- **Masons/Tile Workers** — Tiles chip and crack and so do foundations. Cement, tile, and general masonry work can range from little handyman jobs to issues that can threaten the stability and livability of your property.

- **Landscapers/Gardeners** — Curb appeal is important, especially if your building is located on a street with other units competing for renters. Landscaping and ongoing gardening are a great way to keep your vacancy rates down and your property value up.

- **Pest Control** — This is a big deal. Cockroaches and ants can drive tenants away quickly. Get a reliable pest control service, and sign up for ongoing maintenance.

- **Regional Services** — Depending on your property's location, you may want to add additional services such as snow removal, air conditioning repair, pool services, etc.

- **Carpenters** — Many people think carpenters work only with wood. Not true. Carpenters work with a variety of materials to build, remodel, retrofit, maintain and repair your investment property.

Also ask the seller who he or she has been using for each service and if they would recommend that particular service provider. If you get a solid recommendation from the previous owner, that service provider may be your best bet since they will already have first-hand knowledge of the property and may also be aware of any pre-existing issues.

The next few pages are designed to help you keep track of your referrals and your experiences with each service provider. Problems arise when you least expect it. Take good notes, and keep this book handy. If you are self managing, you will want the plumber's number close by for that inevitable 3:00 a.m. clogged-toilet call.

The following pages contain a homework assignment. Start asking for referrals and keep this list handy and updated either in this book, or better yet, saved to cloud space. Visit www.DestinationPerpetuity.com for all the free, downloadable forms you need.

With properties I self manage, I give my tenants the 24-hour number of my preferred plumbing company. If there is any issue, they call the plumbing company directly. I have an understanding with all of my tenants that the plumber will fix the problem and then bill the appropriate party. If the pipes are broken or rusted, I get the bill. If the plumber finds bottle caps or clumps of hair in the drain, the tenant gets the bill. Best of all, I never get a 3:00 a.m. call.

Plumbers

Referral #1:

Contact information:

State license#:

Worker's comp insurance company:

Policy #:

Bond company:

Policy #:

Referred by:

Notes:

Referral #2:

Contact information:

State license#:

Worker's comp insurance company:

Policy #:

Bond company:

Policy #:

Referred by:

Notes:

Mason / Tile Workers

Referral #1:

Contact information:

State license#:

Worker's comp insurance company:

Policy #:

Bond company:

Policy #:

Referred by:

Notes:

Referral #2:

Contact information:

State license#:

Worker's comp insurance company:

Policy #:

Bond company:

Policy #:

Referred by:

Notes:

Referral #1:

Contact information:

State license#:

Worker's comp insurance company:

Policy #:

Bond company:

Policy #:

Referred by:

Notes:

Referral #2:

Contact information:

State license#:

Worker's comp insurance company:

Policy #:

Bond company:

Policy #:

Referred by:

Notes:

Electricians

Referral #1:

Contact information:

State license#:

Worker's comp insurance company:

Policy #:

Bond company:

Policy #:

Referred by:

Notes:

Referral #2:

Contact information:

State license#:

Worker's comp insurance company:

Policy #:

Bond company:

Policy #:

Referred by:

Notes:

General Handyman

Referral #1:

Contact information:

State license#:

Worker's comp insurance company:

Policy #:

Bond company:

Policy #:

Referred by:

Notes:

Referral #2:

Contact information:

State license#:

Worker's comp insurance company:

Policy #:

Bond company:

Policy #:

Referred by:

Notes:

Carpenters

Referral #1:

Contact information:

State license#:

Worker's comp insurance company:

Policy #:

Bond company:

Policy #:

Referred by:

Notes:

Referral #2:

Contact information:

State license#:

Worker's comp insurance company:

Policy #:

Bond company:

Policy #:

Referred by:

Notes:

 Roofers

Referral #1:

Contact information:

State license#:

Worker's comp insurance company:

Policy #:

Bond company:

Policy #:

Referred by:

Notes:

Roofers

Referral #2:

Contact information:

State license#:

Worker's comp insurance company:

Policy #:

Bond company:

Policy #:

Referred by:

Notes:

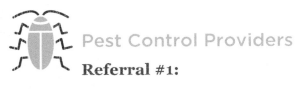

Pest Control Providers

Referral #1:

Contact information:

State license#:

Worker's comp insurance company:

Policy #:

Bond company:

Policy #:

Referred by:

Notes:

Pest Control Providers

Referral #2:

Contact information:

State license#:

Worker's comp insurance company:

Policy #:

Bond company:

Policy #:

Referred by:

Notes:

Referral #1:

Contact information:

State license#:

Worker's comp insurance company:

Policy #:

Bond company:

Policy #:

Referred by:

Notes:

Referral #2:

Contact information:

State license#:

Worker's comp insurance company:

Policy #:

Bond company:

Policy #:

Referred by:

Notes:

Carpet / Drapery Cleaners

Referral #1:

Contact information:

State license#:

Worker's comp insurance company:

Policy #:

Bond company:

Policy #:

Referred by:

Notes:

Carpet / Drapery Cleaners

Referral #2:

Contact information:

State license#:

Worker's comp insurance company:

Policy #:

Bond company:

Policy #:

Referred by:

Notes:

Landscapers / Gardeners

Referral #1:

Contact information:

State license#:

Worker's comp insurance company:

Policy #:

Bond company:

Policy #:

Referred by:

Notes:

Landscapers / Gardeners

Referral #2:

Contact information:

State license#:

Worker's comp insurance company:

Policy #:

Bond company:

Policy #:

Referred by:

Notes:

Regional Services

Referral #1:

Contact information:

State license#:

Worker's comp insurance company:

Policy #:

Bond company:

Policy #:

Referred by:

Notes:

Referral #2:

Contact information:

State license#:

Worker's comp insurance company:

Policy #:

Bond company:

Policy #:

Referred by:

Notes:

Tales from the Road
Travelogue #4
Pick me, I'm #1!

Joe decided to become a real estate baron. His friend Michael was making a killing flipping houses, and although Joe did not know anything about real estate, he did know one thing for certain; he was much smarter than Michael. If Michael could do it, he could do it better. Joe searched the local paper and found the agent who claimed to be both the #1 agent and local expert. He made the call and explained that he was ready to start flipping houses. His agent assured him he had made the right call and told him about an amazing deal that was about to come on the market. The agent explained he had just gotten the listing and that no one else knew about it. He told Joe it would move fast, and if Joe was a serious investor, this was absolutely the deal to start with.

The pro forma numbers the agent presented to Joe indicated amazing upside potential. Joe's new agent assured him if he got the rents up and did a little paint and carpet fix-up, Joe could flip the property quickly and make a killing. Joe was eager to begin his new career. Although both the price of the property and the down payment were substantiality higher than Joe had originally wanted to spend, Joe's agent assured him it was a great investment and if he hesitated, it would be gone. Joe instructed his agent to write an offer; after just two counter offers, he had the property under contract. When the transaction entered the appraisal phase, Joe was shocked that the property did not appraise for the sale price. Joe's agent, Michael, continued to tout the pro forma numbers on this deal, pointing out that the rents were absurdly low and backing up his statement by showing Joe ads for other similar rental properties in the area that charged much higher rent. Joe felt confident in working with the #1 agent and decided to take his agent's advice. He accessed a line of credit on his home to make up the difference on the appraisal, thereby falling within the underwriters' lending requirements. Joe closed escrow on the property and planned to raise rents quickly to what he had been told was market value. His plan was to use the increased cash flow to pay off the line of credit quickly and be profitable in a very short time. Instead, Joe came to find out that the building he purchased was under rent control, and although his agent was correct in stating the units were *under market*, Joe was extremely limited in how and when he could raise rents. Joe was able to raise the rents over time, but the process took years not months.

Rules of the Road

Rule #4
Do your homework, and get referrals.

Buying real estate is not only the best way, the quickest way, the safest way, but the only way to become wealthy.

Marshall Field

Chapter 5
Picking the Right Property

"A straight path never leads anywhere except to the objective."
– Andre Gide

Now, you might be asking yourself how is it that we are more than half way through the book and we are just now getting around to the discussion of property selection? The answer is simple. Preparation is the key to any successful journey.

Locating and purchasing the right property takes patience, and although the road to financial freedom can seem long and a bit bumpy, the destination of *Perpetuity* is well worth the time and minor inconveniences. Keep in mind that this is not just an investment for you, but also ideally one that will flourish for generations to come. If you stick to the plan and encourage your heirs to do so as well, great grandchildren that you may never meet will be singing your praises. Such a journey must be planned very carefully.

Okay, so you've done your research, selected your team, and you are ready to roll. Time to start shopping!

Let's first review the three rules of real estate: "Location, location, location." I am sure you have heard this old adage many times, but it is important to understand the actual nuances of this timeless advice.

Location

Properties can be rehabbed, curb appeal can be reworked, and additional square footage can be added, but the location your building sits on will never change. If you are unfamiliar with the neighborhood, make sure your real estate agent clearly understands the subtleties of the area. I cannot stress how vital location is to successful income property ownership.

If the property is located in an area that is undergoing re-urbanization, that could spell increased rents in the near future and market appreciation for years to come. If the area is blighted and the property sits behind a train track or just under a freeway off ramp, the opposite could be true.

Not all income-producing properties are good investments, even at a bargain price. If your property is adjacent to a smelting factory with a horrible down-wind stench, that is what we call a negative *material fact*. Location can greatly impact marketability, cash flow, and future appreciation. You will most likely have a harder time getting and keeping tenants with any noticeable challenge such as a neighboring fish cannery or a correctional institution. Does that make the property a bad investment? Not necessarily. It's just one aspect of the property that has to be looked at in the overall consideration. If the price is right and the rent rolls show a clear history of steady cash flow, perhaps that property should remain on the list regardless of the wafting tuna smell or possible nearby prison breaks.

Oftentimes, properties that are less desirable will have greater cash flow, but such a property may also have a lesser chance for appreciation. All the pros and cons need to be considered. This is where your trusted travel partners come in and guide you. The comparable sales or the *comps* don't lie, so review the information carefully, and you will quickly come to see why the right properties go for a premium price. This is where you and your real estate agent will need to review your goals. When I meet with a new client who is looking for their first investment property, one of the first questions I ask is: "Do you want cash flow or potential appreciation?"

Most everyone has the same answer: "Both!"

Well, you can have both; however, most properties that offer strong cap rates up front have less potential for appreciation and vice versa. Why? Because properties in more-desirable areas can be marketed with a less-desirable gross multiplier.

This is why you must clearly define your goals. Your real estate agent's local market knowledge coupled with the historical data of the comparable properties and the current rental conditions in the area will help answer the question. Bottom line — each property must be considered in light of a variety of these location-related factors.

Condition of the Property

As we discussed in chapter 2, there are many factors that come into play when determining the value of a property. If the listing agent understands the appropriate way to price a property, the building condition should have already been taken into consideration, and much of the heavy lifting is done.

As an astute buyer, you will need to factor in property condition as a major element when writing an offer and negotiating a sale price. This is where your team can be invaluable. When it is obvious that the property is going to need a new roof, for instance, if that cost was not factored into the list price, you and your agent may decide to adjust the purchase offer accordingly to help offset the cost of future repairs. If your agent has a good standing relationship with a roofer, get a reliable *ballpark* figure on what the roof repair is going to cost. You and your agent can then use that knowledge to explain, in part, why you arrived at the offer being presented. Such information can aid you in negotiating a more favorable purchase price.

TRAVEL TIP

Risk can equal reward. To attract potential buyers, less-desirable properties will typically be marketed and sold at a price that offers a more-desirable gross rent multiplier.

This is yet another opportunity for agents to prove they know their stuff. The really good agents will know what the current rents should be in the area and provide that information for your consideration. It is not uncommon to find a building with rents below market. A sharp agent will recognize these opportunities. It takes an agent that understands the business of income-producing properties to identify and negotiate the right deal.

Purchasing income-producing real estate with below-market rents, in non rent-controlled markets, allows you over time the opportunity of raising the rents to fair market values, which will improve your gross multiplier and thereby raise the value of your property and equity.

Most investors shy away from buildings with rent controls in place. Areas governed by strict rent control policies can make it very difficult for the owner to keep pace with market rents. Oftentimes, a building in a rent-controlled area will seem like a bargain. To entice prospective buyers, a listing agent may present the property showing *pro forma* rents. This is not an uncommon practice, and despite the listing agent clearly stating that the rents are *projections* you are still dealing with what looks good on paper. Even when you find a non rent-controlled building with rents far below market rates, you might not be able to raise the rents right away. Oftentimes, the current tenants have a lease in place, and the rents cannot be raised until the lease is finished. Some leases allow for renewals at a pre-set dollar amount for years to come. You will have an opportunity to review the leases during your due-diligence period so that you understand your obligations once you take title. You need to know how state and local laws will affect your ability to manage your property. Understanding how and when you can raise the rents is key to creating a profitable income property.

By now, you understand how rental income not only determines your cash flow, but how it also in large part determines property value. With a fixed interest rate and your expenses under control, simply raising your rents by two or three percent annually can greatly increase your cash flow and raise the value of your property within a relatively short period of time. A well-run property should keep pace with inflation. This is another good argument for professional property management. If you are managing your own property, you run the risk of becoming friendly with your tenants and softhearted about rental increases. Don't put your self and your investment return at risk. Let the property manager run your building as a business to maximize your return.

TRAVEL
TIP

What's the local economy like? Along with "location, location, location," let's add "jobs, jobs, jobs." If you are in an area with a solid, growing economy, the jobs will bring tenants. Supply and demand. Look for an area that has a well-established industry. In Southern California, we have the film industry in Hollywood and the aerospace industry in the South Bay. Those industries have been mainstays of the economy, and income-producing properties in those areas are heavily sought after, making vacancy rarely an issue.

Vacancy

A vacant unit is a landlord's worst enemy. A good property management company should be able to keep your vacancies to a minimum. To give you an idea of how vacancy affects your bottom line, let's look at two scenarios:

- You own a 3-unit building, and you have one vacancy. One-third of your cash has just stopped flowing.

- You own a 10-unit building with one vacancy. One-tenth of your cash has just stopped flowing.

Although larger buildings will have more maintenance issues due to more square footage and more tenants, they are typically a safer investment since the vacancy factor is easier to absorb.

TRAVEL TIP

Keeping your vacancies low not only ensures your cash flow, it also maintains the rental history value of your building should you decide at some point to trade or sell the property. Books and records that reflect low to no-vacancy rates garner a premium from potential buyers.

Unit Mix

In most markets, a two or three-bedroom apartment with two or more bathrooms is typically the ideal rental product. If you happen to be in a college town that lacks student housing, perhaps studios are the hot commodities. As always, look to your team, your property manager, and your real estate agent for their areas of expertise on what will be the most desirable types of units.

Utilities

Ideally, you will want to look for units that have individual utility meters, which typically means that the tenants pay their own utilities. If your building is *master-metered*, you as the owner will pay all utilities. If at all possible, try to find buildings with separate meters where the tenants pay their own gas and electric. If you carry the responsibility of those utility costs, it becomes difficult to project and control your expenses. I once owned a master-metered, 20-unit building in Phoenix, and I dreaded the summer months. My electric bill often tripled due to AC usage, and my cash flow quickly evaporated from May to August.

Parking

Good parking can be crucial. So much so that some lenders will not lend on a building without parking. Here again, it is important to know your local market. If your building caters to a demographic that typically uses mass transit and a public facility is within walking distance, a building without parking may be an acceptable choice if the numbers make sense and the lender approves.

Amenities

Does your new building have a pool? In a desert community, it is a must to attract tenants, but if you are in a more temperate climate, the pool may become more of a liability than an asset due to insurance and maintenance issues.

Gym facilities, BBQ areas, clubhouses, tennis courts, pools, and spas tend to attract lifestyle renters. The more you have to offer, the more interest you will have in your property. Washers and dryers in a unit are gold. However, a laundry room is often an acceptable choice. A building with no laundry facilities whatsoever is cause for concern.

Good light is also an amenity. Studies have shown that most renters make their decision to rent within the first minute of being inside a property. Good light is very important. Few tenants want to live in a dark unit.

TRAVEL

TIP

Ask yourself this simple question: "Would I want to live here?" Light, bright, and airy is always a winner.

Deferred Maintenance

Unforeseen deferred maintenance can greatly lengthen the time it takes for you to reach your goal — a life with a cash flow in *Perpetuity*. Careful inspections by you, your property inspector, real estate agent, and property manager can save big bucks before and after you take ownership. You want as many expert eyes on the property as possible before selecting the one that you want to purchase. Due-diligence inspections are extremely important during this time. Weed out the money pits, and stay focused on the cash cows.

You will, of course, want to have a clear understanding of the overall building condition and be cognizant of the current and potential maintenance needs.

Be especially mindful of the big-ticket items: the roof, plumbing, foundation, termite damage, HVAC units, paint, flooring, appliances, asphalt, chimneys, and electrical. Use these tips below to gain a better understanding of what the overall maintenance picture for the property might be.

The Roof — Most property inspectors will give you an view of the current condition, and can also estimate the remaining useful life of the current roof. A damaged roof or one near the end of its useful life can be a maintenance nightmare. When calculating the cost of a roof replacement, make sure to include the cost of relocating your tenants during the repairs. Depending on the size of the building, your temporary relocation costs could be more than the cost of a new roof.

Plumbing — Be careful of older buildings that have galvanized plumbing, which tends to be problematic. Leaks and broken pipes are all too common. PVC is a better choice, and copper plumbing is the best. A large percentage of your ongoing maintenance will be water related. Make sure you check the pipes and sewer line. I highly recommend that you have the sewer scoped. Scoping a sewer line is well worth the cost. If there is an issue, you need to know about it during the due-diligence period. The last thing you want is a backed-up sewer on your newly purchased property.

Foundation — This is a big one. A faulty foundation can be an enormous expense. With older buildings, I will often bring in a foundation specialist. It is money well spent to know your building is or is not on solid ground before signing off on your inspection contingency.

Termite Damage — It's a common problem and can be a big-ticket item in a sales transaction. Typically, the seller will pay for most if not all of the termite work; however, that needs to be negotiated within the inspection period.

TRAVEL TIP

Make sure you insist on the seller using a licensed, bonded, and insured termite company. Also, ask about the company's work guarantees (typically 12 months after the date of the clearance) before agreeing on the seller's choice of termite companies. If termites show back up in a couple months, you will want to know you are covered.

HVAC Units — Older furnaces and air conditioning units can be problematic, expensive to repair, and costly to maintain and operate. If the unit is in need of repair, try to negotiate a new replacement unit prior to the close of the transaction. You will be glad you did when summer comes.

Paint — If you do not think that paint is a big deal, you are wrong. Not only does paint add curb appeal, it also helps protects your structure from the elements. Painting a large apartment building inside and out can be a costly venture. Look closely. If the paint is peeling or the stucco is flaking, get a bid before you sign off on your property inspection.

TRAVEL TIP

Keep your buildings clean and well maintained. Fresh paint, clean carpet, and a little landscaping will help ensure that you grab the prime tenants. And don't discount curb appeal. You can have the nicest interiors in town, but if the curb appeal does not work, prospective tenants won't even get out of the car to see the unit. Don't forget about the human element of your new business. Stand in front of your building, and ask yourself, "Would I live here?"

Flooring — If your building has carpet, you will inherit the cost of cleaning or replacement with each new tenant. Hardwood floors are typically preferable. They are generally more durable and more appealing to most renters than carpeting, and they are easier and less costly for landlords to maintain.

Always check under the carpet. Many carpeted properties have hardwood floors just waiting to be rediscovered and refinished. Oftentimes, landlords will carpet rather than redo hardwood floors as a quick fix. Pulling back old carpeting and discovering hidden hardwood floors is like finding a vein of gold. Sanding and varnishing hardwood can be costly, but units with hardwood floors typically garner higher rents than carpeted apartments. Bottom line — the investment is worth the long-term increase in cash flow.

Appliances — If the current owner owns the appliances, you are most likely buying them with the building, but don't make that assumption or take the word of the listing agent. Make certain your real estate agent requests the appliances in the offer and then double check with the estoppels to make sure everyone is in agreement on the ownership of the appliances.

Look into getting a home warranty as part of your purchase agreement. Oftentimes, the seller will pay for this service. A good home warranty from a reputable company with the correct coverage can save you thousands of dollars in repairs and appliance replacement costs. Your agent most likely has a home warranty company that he/she will recommend. Make sure you take the time to speak with the home warranty representative and get the proper coverage for your property. Not all home warranties are created equal, and not all home warranty companies are easy to deal with. Before agreeing to a home warranty company, do some home work — check Yelp reviews or better yet get a referral — and save yourself grief and cash.

Asphalt — Parking areas are often overlooked. Make sure to notice the condition of the driveway. Cracks and potholes may mean a slurry seal needs to be done. This is a sizable expense and one that needs to be factored in, as does the inconvenience it may cost the tenants. Better to do it before you take ownership. Request that the seller take on the repair and deal with the headaches of tenant complaints prior to the close of the transaction.

Chimneys — If your building has wood-burning fireplaces, beware. A fireplace is often a sought-after amenity that will help you attract potential renters, but chimneys that have not been maintained can have build-ups of creosote, and that can be a fire hazard. Chimney inspections can be expensive, but uncovering these issues is well worth the time and the cost. The knowledge of any such issue in your due-diligence period allows you the opportunity of remediating the issue with the seller as opposed to working with an insurance company and attorneys after a fire.

Electrical — Be careful here, electrical repair bills can be shocking! If you get a heads up of an electrical issue during the due-diligence inspection period, try to get the seller to take care of the issue before the close of the transaction. Electrical issues are not only expensive, they can also be very dangerous. Bad wiring is a ticking time bomb. If you can't negotiate to have the work done prior to taking ownership, then make sure you have budgeted to do the work as quickly as possible.

Cash Flow

Cash flow is the primary reason you are taking this journey, so it is extremely important that you understand how dollars get spent and more importantly how dollars can be saved. Keep in mind that there is no set cap rate or GRM that is the right number. Several contributing factors come into play. The location of the property and the income the property generates are two of the most important factors. However, you will need an alert agent to truly zero-in on the actual cash flow potential of the properties you are considering.

TRAVEL TIP

A property with obvious deferred maintenance might be a diamond in the rough. Many investors will shy away from such properties, but an astute investor with an eye for a building with "good bones" in a promising area can cash in with a well-thought-out, and properly executed rehab plan.

Due Diligence

Every offer you write should include a *due-diligence* period. This is the time frame in which you and your team will review and inspect any and all information pertinent to the sale of the property you are contracted to purchase. Most due-diligence reviews focus primarily on two areas:

1. **The books and records of the property** (rents, expenses, cash flow)

2. **The physical condition of the property**

This is not to say there are not other areas of concern to be examined within your due-diligence period. Each transaction is unique and may have unique due-diligence issues; however, books and records and the physical inspection are the two most common and arguably the most important elements. Let's take a closer look at how this process takes place. Lets start with the money.

During your due-diligence period, you will have the opportunity to review the owner's books and records. If you were presented with actual rents in the listing presentation, this is your opportunity to review that information and cross-check it with the estoppels provided by the tenants. Your agent and your lender should also be double-checking this information. Your due-diligence period is your opportunity to better understand what you are buying and verify that the information you were given when you wrote the offer is accurate. Expenses can vary greatly and can fluctuate wildly from year to year. Reviewing the property's financial history as far back as the owner has records allows you a better understanding of what you are buying. The better you understand the current books, records, and cash flow, the better you will understand what return to anticipate. The books and records can also help you to better understand the physical condition of your new property. Say for instance you find the foundation has been repaired three times in the last 10 years. That would be a huge red flag to me, and I would want to add a foundation expert to my inspection team before signing off on my physical inspection.

The overall physical condition of the property is of vital importance. You will have a due-diligence period for the physical inspection that may or may not be the same time frame as the review of books and records. It is important to inspect the building and review the inspectors' findings as soon as possible. If there are items of concern that were not originally disclosed, you may want to ask the seller to replace or repair the issues of concern. Oftentimes, a credit or a price reduction are given in lieu of repairs. Whatever the case, you will want to come to terms with the seller on any and all issues of concern before removing your appropriate contingencies of sale.

Because due-diligence is vital to properly understanding the cash flow and financial viability of your investment property, I have compiled a basic due-diligence form that appears on pages 164 through 175. Make several copies, and expand on it based on each individual property you review. You will want a fresh due-diligence record for each property. Keep each form handy for reference. This form is also available as a free download at www.DestinationPerpetuity.com.

TRAVEL
TIP

When you first discover an issue during the due-diligence period, it becomes a "material fact" about the property. Asking the seller to either repair the issue, offer a credit in lieu of repair, or re-trading the deal are all reasonable responses to such a discovery. The seller can choose to resolve the issue, offer a credit or take no action — all are acceptable responses. The seller's agent knows that, should you decide not to buy the building because of this newly discovered issue, the owner is required to disclose the issue to the next buyer. That next buyer would likely have the same concerns and typically seek the same remediation, credit, or reduced sale price. With that knowledge, the issue is often addressed and hopefully can be remedied to the buyer's satisfaction so that the transaction can proceed. Bottom line: don't be afraid to ask.

Remember there is no perfect property — even brand new buildings have issues. The key to a successful due-diligence process is mitigating as many issues as possible and having the knowledge of and accepting the responsibility for any issue that could not be resolved with the seller prior to the close of the transaction.

As you begin to review buildings for consideration, try to answer as many of these questions as possible before making an offer. You will not always be able to get all of this information from every listing before writing the offer, but the more informed you are before writing the offer, the better. Remember, information is power, so be powerful.

Due-Diligence Record

Property address: _____

_____

_____

_____

Property APN number: _____

Year built: _____ Gross building area: _____

# of units/floors: _____ Elevator: _____ Yes _____ No

Age: _____ Condition: _____

Utility meters: _____ Master metered: _____ Individually metered

Individual water heaters: _____

Is there a resident manager? _____ Yes _____ No

Compensation (rent and/or salary?): _____

What are the resident manager's duties?

_____

_____

_____

_____

_____

_____

_____

_____

_____

_____

_____

_____

_____

_____

Due-Diligence Record

Section B: Neighborhood, Property, and Area Summary

Neighborhood	Good	Average	Fair	Poor
Employment Stability (Local)				
Overall Livability				
Quality of Construction				
Room Size and Layout				
Adequacy of Shopping Facilities				
Adequacy of Utilities				
Police and Fire Protection				
Recreational Facilities				
Property Compatibility				
General Appearance of Properties				
Appeal to Market				
Property	**Good**	**Average**	**Fair**	**Poor**
Architectural Attractiveness				
Landscaping				
Protection from Detrimental Conditions				
Condition of Exterior				
Condition of Interior				
Adequacy of Public Transportation				
Closets and Storage				
Light and Ventilation				
Convenience to Employment Centers				
Compatibility to Neighborhood				
Overall Appeal and Marketability				

Due-Diligence Record

Area Data

Access / Convenience Item	Distance From Subject Property	Good	Average	Fair	Poor
Public Transportation					
Employment Centers					
Shopping Facilities					
Schools					
Freeway Access					

General Comments including either favorable or unfavorable elements not mentioned (e.g., public parks, view, noise, parking congestion)

_____

_____

_____

_____

_____

_____

_____

_____

_____

_____

_____

_____

_____

_____

_____

Due-Diligence Record

Amenities

Property	UNIT
❏ Clubhouse	❏ Refrigerator
❏ Jacuzzi	❏ Oven/Range
❏ Exercise Facility	❏ Microwave
❏ Storage Areas	❏ Washer/Dryer
❏ Swimming Pool	❏ Hookups
❏ Basketball Courts	❏ Trash Compactor
❏ Playground	❏ Fireplace
❏ Sauna	❏ Vaulted Ceilings
❏ Tennis Courts	❏ Ceiling Fans
❏ Laundry Rooms	❏ Window Covering
❏ Racquetball Court	❏ Lofts
❏ Volleyball Court	❏ Internet
❏ Billiards Room	❏ A/C
❏ Elevators	❏ Storage
❏ Secured Access	❏ Balcony/Patio
❏ Walking/Jogging	❏ Dishwasher
❏ Business Center	❏ Cable TV Ready
❏ Carports	❏ Vertical Blinds
❏ Picnic Areas	❏ Mini Blinds
❏ Garages	❏ Drapes
❏ Car Wash Area	❏ Security Systems
❏ Barbecue Areas	❏ Disposal
❏ Sprinkler System	❏ Smoke / CO Detectors
❏ Other	❏ Other
_____	_____
_____	_____

Comments: _____

_____

_____

_____

Due-Diligence Record

Annual gross scheduled income: $_____

Annual proforma income: $_____

Is the building under rent controls? _____ Yes _____ No

Terms: _____

_____

_____

Are there any commercial tenants? _____ Yes_____ No

Type of business: _____

_____

Does the current owner offer move-in specials?___Yes ___No

If so, describe:_____

_____

Vacancies

How many units are currently vacant?_____

How many vacant units are in "rent-ready" condition? _____

How many units have been vacant in previous 3 years? _____

Reason for vacancy: _____

_____

_____

On-site Laundry (if applicable)

How many washers and dryers?_____ washers _____ dryers

Owned by: _____ landlord _____ vendor

Laundry Income: $_____

Comments: _____

_____

_____

Due-Diligence Record

You will need to review the current operating expenses along with the rent rolls from Section C on the previous page. Try to get as many years' worth of expenses as possible. You should review a minimum of three years of records to get as clear an understanding of your potential investment as possible.

Use the following worksheet to summarize the expense picture for this property.

Expense Worksheet

Expense Type	Current Year Amount (based on estimated purchase price)	Previous Year Amount (actual)	Amount for Two Years Ago (actual)	Notes
Mortgage				
Taxes				
Insurance				
Management				
• Property Mgmt. Company Fee				
• Resident Manager (rent and/or salary)				
• Other Payroll Expense (describe in Notes)				
Landscape Service				
Pool Service				
Elevator Service				
Utilities (paid for by):				
• Gas Tenant Landlord				
• Water Tenant Landlord				
• Electric Tenant Landlord				
• Sewer Tenant Landlord				
• Trash Pick Up Tenant Landlord				
Repairs & Maintenance				

Due-Diligence Record

In this section, complete the information regarding property condition, and list the capital improvements and replacements for at least the prior three years (or longer if the records are available).

Describe, in general, the current condition and history of property:

_____

_____

_____

_____

_____

Foundation and Structure
What is the condition of the foundation and structure?

_____

_____

_____

Is the property on a raised foundation?

_____

_____

_____

Are there any substandard notices from the city?

_____

_____

_____

Parking/Paving

What type of off-street parking does the property have?

Garage? _____Yes _____No _____Number of garages

Fire sprinklers? _____Yes _____No Lot?_____Yes_____No

Number of covered spaces _____

Number of uncovered spaces _____

Total number of spaces per unit _____

Number of additional spaces _____

What is the condition of paved surfaces
(drives, sidewalks, parking lots)?

_____

_____

_____

Roof

What type is the roof?_____

What is the condition of the roof?

_____

_____

_____

Utilities

Is the cooking gas or electric? _____

What is the condition of the electrical system?

_____

_____

_____

Type of wiring: _____

Is there any unsafe wiring present?_____Yes _____No

Are there any code violations? _____Yes_____No

What is the condition of the plumbing?

_____

_____

_____

Is the pipe galvanized, PVC, or copper? _____

What percentage of each? _____

Are there any code violations? _____Yes _____No

Safety

Do units have fire sprinklers? _____Yes _____No

Are smoke/CO detectors battery or hard wired? _____

What is the type and condition of exterior lighting?

_____

_____

_____

Are there security systems in place? If so, describe:

_____

_____

Is there a pool?____ Yes____No Is it fenced?____ Yes____No

Paint (or other finishes):

If built before 1979, has there been a lead-based paint

inspection? _____

Results:

_____

What is the condition of the interior and exterior paint or

other finishes?

_____

_____

Capital Improvements

Describe any capital improvements/replacements made to the property for the prior three years (or longer if records are available).

Appliance replacement/repair:

_____

_____

_____

Painting:

_____

_____

_____

Carpet:

_____

_____

_____

Electrical:

_____

_____

_____

Plumbing:

_____

_____

_____

Window covering:

_____

_____

_____

Landscape:

_____

_____

Pool:

_____

_____

HVAC units:

_____

_____

Lighting:

_____

_____

Paving:

_____

_____

Other (please describe):

_____

_____

_____

_____

_____

Don't Forget the Money

This journey is all about the dollars: If the numbers or the potential numbers don't work, it's the wrong building! Your accountant can do the fancy math and show you how owning income property will affect your tax returns. However, for a quick blanket look at what you are buying, you can apply a simple formula. Let's say you are buying a property for $1,000,000 with 30 percent down and a 30-year loan at 4 percent interest. Here is what your transaction will look like in an income analysis breakdown:

Start with the purchase price	**$1,000,000**
Minus off the down payment	$300,000
Leaving you the loan amount	$700,000
Next:	
Take your gross schedule income (or pro forma)	$100,000
Subtract the annual vacancy allowance (5%)	$5,000
Giving you the gross operating income	$95,000
Subtract the operating expenses	$28,500
Leaving you with the net operating income	$66,500

The amount you pay for the property, the amount of your loan balance, and the amount of your interest rate are the upfront variables that will determine your return on cash. These numbers will fluctuate as rents and expenses change.

Obviously, the more cash you put down, the better your cash flow; however, high down payments are not always the best use of funds. Leveraging purchase allows you to free up cash and possibly purchase additional properties. I always suggest consulting a CPA to help determine how much cash to put into a down payment.

The following pages give you three examples of an income analysis based on the previous scenario with variables for down payments and purchase price.

Scenario #1 – all cash, 100 % down:

PROJECTED INCOME ANALYSIS

Property Address:	123 Main St. Perpetuity USA
Purchase Price:	$1,000,000
Down Payment:	$1,000,000 (Based on = 100%)
Loan Amount:	$0
Gross Scheduled Income:	$100,000
Vacancy Allowance:	$5,000 (Based on = 5%)
Gross Operating Income:	$95,000
Operating Expenses:	$28,500
Net Operating Income:	$66,500
Loan Payment:	$0 (Based on = 0.00%)

GROSS SPENDABLE INCOME:	$66,500
Return On Cash (percentage)	**6.65**
Gross Rent Multiplier	**10.00**
CAP Rate	**6.65**

Scenario #2 - 50% down:

PROJECTED INCOME ANALYSIS

Property Address:	123 Main St. Perpetuity USA
Purchase Price:	$1,000,000
Down Payment:	$500,000 (Based on = 50%)
Loan Amount:	$500,000
Gross Scheduled Income:	$100,000
Vacancy Allowance:	$5,000 (Based on = 5%)
Gross Operating Income:	$95,000
Operating Expenses:	$28,500
Net Operating Income:	$66,500
Loan Payment:	$ 28,645 (Based on = 4%)

GROSS SPENDABLE INCOME:	**$37,855**
Return On Cash (percentage)	**7.57**
Gross Rent Multiplier	**10.00**
CAP Rate	**6.65**

Notice that the return on cash is affected by the addition of a loan balance, but the GRM and CAP rate are not.

Scenario #3: 50% down, lower purchase price:

PROJECTED INCOME ANALYSIS

Property Address:	123 Main St. Perpetuity USA
Purchase Price:	$900,000
Down Payment:	$450,000 (Based on = 50%)
Loan Amount:	$450,000
Gross Scheduled Income:	$100,000
Vacancy Allowance:	$5,000 (Based on = 5%)
Gross Operating Income:	$95,000
Operating Expenses:	$28,500
Net Operating Income:	$66,500
Loan Payment:	$25,780 (Based on = 4%)

GROSS SPENDABLE INCOME:	$40,420
Return On Cash (percentage)	**9.05**
Gross Rent Multiplier	**9.00**
CAP Rate	**7.39**

Notice in this scenario with a reduction in price, the return on cash is increased, the GRM goes down and the CAP rate goes up.

Tales from the Road

Travelogue #5
*Take a Walk on the Sunny Side
of the Street.*

In 1964, Betty and her husband Robert decided to purchase their first home. They were torn between an 1100 sq. foot house with two bedrooms and 1.5 bathrooms on a 30 x 90 lot in Manhattan Beach just a few blocks from the sand, or a slightly larger 1250 sq. foot property with 3 bedrooms and 1.5 bathrooms on a 50 x 150 lot, a few miles inland in Redondo Beach. They carefully weighed the pros and cons of each purchase. The Manhattan Beach home was priced at $27,000, and the Redondo Beach home was priced at $21,000 — approximately a 30 percent difference in price.

Betty liked the spacious lot in North Redondo Beach, and she liked the idea of the third bedroom. They were planning on having a family, and more bedrooms with a big backyard seemed like a better fit. Robert liked the Manhattan Beach house with its proximity to the ocean. He thought the smaller house was sufficient for their first home, and if the family grew, they could add on a bedroom or even two by adding a second story. Betty argued that a big backyard would be important for children. Robert countered that with the beach just a few blocks away, the smaller house actually had better outdoor space. Betty did not like the coastal fog that rolled in every morning and typically hung around until midday. She said it depressed her, and since she would be staying home with the kids, she wanted to be further inland where sunshine was more consistent. Robert finally relented with a promise from Betty that someday, they would move to a beach cottage after the kids moved out.

Robert and Betty stayed in their 3-bedroom, 1.5-bath home in Redondo Beach for almost 40 years. Robert died in 1996, and his wife Betty died a few years later. I never met either of them, but I heard the story from their son Lawrence who had asked me to sell the house. We listed the Redondo Beach house at $625,000 and received three offers. Shortly after we opened escrow, Lawrence asked me what the little beach cottage his father had wanted would be worth in today's market. All I said was that those properties had shot up quite a bit. I did not have the heart to tell him what he most likely already knew. The little beach cottage was located in a highly desirable area of Manhattan Beach. The land alone in that area was worth nearly $2,000,000.

Rules of the Road

Rule #5

Location, Location, Location.

Buy on the fringe and wait. Buy land near a growing city! Buy real estate when other people want to sell. Hold what you buy!

John Jacob Astor

Chapter 6

Forks in the Road

"By failing to prepare, you are preparing to fail."
– Benjamin Franklin

You need a plan. As Mike Tyson once said, "Everyone has a plan 'til they get punched in the mouth." Don't let the unexpected punch you in the mouth. Start planning now.

This book is your planning guide to financial freedom. Keep it with you, make notes in the margins, get referrals, and make sure nothing gets overlooked. Remember that life is a series of journeys, and being financially secure helps prepare you for both the predictable and the unpredictable twists and turns along your path.

This chapter outlines a few points to ponder. Everyone's journey is a little different. I have listed a few common and not-so-common life events that require thoughtful planning. These forks in the road may or may not be of concern to you, but I guarantee that the unforeseen and the unexpected await you. Plan and prepare for what you can see coming, and then add a little extra for the unknown. Read through my thoughts, and then make a list of your own. It will be time well spent and worthwhile financial planning.

College Tuition

The website *Cynical-C* has reported that, "The cost of a four-year university degree for a child born in 2013 could rise to more than $140,000 due to tuition inflation." That's just for one child. The 2000 census stated, "The  average number of children in U.S. families was 1.86 children." Let's round up and say two kids per family. That's $280,000 to put both your offspring through college. Ouch! Where is that money coming from?

A few years ago, I had a young couple as clients that were looking to buy a starter condo. I suggested instead that they consider purchasing a small duplex. At first they thought it was out of their price range, but when I explained the lender would take a portion of the rent into consideration to offset their income for qualifying, the idea of being landlords blossomed and the couple purchased their first income-producing property. A few years later, they called to tell me they were starting a family and wanted to purchase a "proper home with a yard."

They asked me to sell their duplex and help them find a house. I reminded them of one of the most important rules of real estate: "If possible, Never sell anything!"

Since both partners were working good jobs and had solid FICO scores, they were able to take a small amount of equity from their duplex for the down payment and continue renting the property, while at the same time refinancing the duplex to a 15-year note. I asked why they had chosen the 15-year term. The couple explained that rather than set up a traditional college fund, they had decided to get the duplex paid off three years before the first of their two planned children went off to college. The plan was to pay off the duplex and let the rents from the duplex pay for their children's college tuition.

The duplex was bringing in over $4,000 a month — more than enough to pay the principal, interest, taxes, maintenance, and insurance for the duration of the 15-year loan. Once the loan was paid off, less than one-quarter of that monthly income would be needed for taxes and maintenance, leaving $3,000 a month, or $144,000 over the course of a four-year college education. The theory was that the cost of tuition would rise approximately along the same line as the cost-of-living index and the rental income would ideally keep properly adjusted with the cost of tuition. The couple even went so far as to plan their children three years apart so there would be only one financially painful, overlapping college tuition year when the eldest would be a senior and the youngest a freshman.

Although there are still a few years to go before the kids start college, the plan seems sound as real estate values and rents have for the most part kept up with the cost of education.

Once the children graduate from college, the couple plans to gift the property 50/50 to each child; thus, giving each child the option of a perpetual income stream or a paid-for home to live in. Now, that is sound long-term planning.

Death

What happens if the bread winner dies? Yikes. Not something anybody wants to think about but it happens. I was recently watching a report on CNN examining an unexplainable increase in the mortality rate of middle-aged white Americans. I'm in that demographic,  and although my gene pool says I should be here a nice long time, I think about what would happen to my family if I ceased to be. Although my career income would be lost with my demise, I am comforted to know my real estate portfolio would continue to support my family with or without me.

A few years ago a client of mine suffered a major coronary and died unexpectedly. He was in his mid fifties and by all accounts a relatively healthy man. It was a shocking and horrific time for his family. I spoke to his widow shortly after his death, and she thanked me for having helped them invest wisely with two small income producing properties. The cash flow from those properties helped her and her family maintain their lifestyle and stay in their home.

Economic Downturns

During the great recession one of the few sectors of the economy that stayed strong was income-producing real estate, in particular the multi-family sector. Although the value

of real estate plummeted across the board, apartment building owners found themselves somewhat insulated by and, in some regions, even benefiting from the economic melt down. Why? As people lost their homes, they turned to multifamily housing and, in some areas, landlords were able to ask for higher rents. This simple example of supply and demand is one reason why apartment buildings are to some extent considered recession proof.

Family Matters

In my world, nothing matters more than my family and nothing costs more money. "Keeping up with the Joneses" is expensive enough, but when your child's 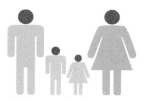 high school band wins the state championships and they are invited to the nationals in Hawaii, you can say Aloha to your savings account.

How about my client who had a difficult time conceiving, and after a visit the fertility client ended up with triplets. Yikes!

We baby boomers are also sometimes referred to as the "Sandwich Generation" — those of us not only raising our children but also looking after our aging parents. If your parents did not properly prepare for their own retirement, you may find yourself making up the ever-increasing divide between cost of living in our inflationary economy and their fixed income.

A few years back, one of my long-time clients, Alan, lost his father. His mother was in relatively good health, but she was beginning to get confused and anxious about being alone.

She refused to move in with her son, as she did not want to be a burden. Alan contacted me and asked how we could restructure his real estate portfolio to earmark money in the event his mother would need to be placed in a care facility. He wanted only the best for his mother, and the cost of the facility he liked was over $5,000 a month.

After a quick review of his portfolio, it became clear that the equity in his mountain hideaway cabin in Big Bear, which he rarely visited, had the capacity to generate a great deal more cash flow than the random dollars the vacation rental company generated. The property was put on the market and quickly went under contract.

The cabin was not sold but exchanged via IRS 1031 for a like-kind property. Both were income-producing properties, but the triplex he traded into produced four times more income than the ski lodge he rarely used. Although he no longer had the bragging rights of a mountain hideaway, he now had the comfort and security of the cash flow needed to set his mother up in a five-star facility for as long as she would live.

Alan is a relatively young man in his fifties, but he plans to keep this same income-producing property and use the cash flow for any of his or his wife's long-term care costs so as not to burden his own children. The property will then pass to his children upon his death so that they can use the income for any of their needs. By the way, Alan still visits the same hideaway cabin he used to own; he just rents it once or twice a year now from the new owner without the worry or concerns with mortgage and maintenance.

Health Care

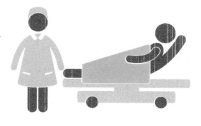

Life is full of surprises and one of the most unwelcome is unexpected health issues. The cost of health care is skyrocketing and even if you have insurance, deductible and items not covered by health care plans can devastate your bank account. A trip to the emergency room for a broken leg can be even more devastating to your wallet than the snapped femur that landed you there.

Job Loss

I think one of the biggest lessons from the great recession was that employment is a privilege. When the economy shrank, jobs evaporated. As a real estate agent, my cash flow changed dramatically as the economy melted. What stayed strong in my financial world was my income-producing real estate. It was my security blanket in an otherwise bleak financial time.

Legal Fees

Ever get sued? Its no fun, and it can be very expensive. I once had a client that was sued by a neighbor for rebuilding a fence on a property line after it fell down in a windstorm. The fence was rebuilt exactly

where it had been for over 60 years; however, the neighbor, who did not even live on the property, claimed the stress of her neighbor rebuilding the fence caused her emotional trauma, eventually leading to brain tumors. WHAT?!?!?!? She wanted the fence removed and tens of thousands of dollars in punitive damages. WHAT?!?!?!?

How can this be, you ask? Answer, in California anybody can sue anybody for just about anything. Absurd? You bet, the bottom line is crazy people get crazy ideas and decide to sue for crazy reasons. You can't plan for such things directly but you can plan indirectly by having a source of excess cash flow.

Travel

Enough with the doom-and-gloom stuff. You need to have a little fun along the way and travel can put a smile on your  face but also a dent in your budget. A trip to overseas is expensive. Really expensive if you do it right. Lets face it a budget hotel in Budapest is not what you want for your European getaway.

Here are some key words for travel planning:

- Business Class

- Five Star

- Down Comforters

- Feather Pillows

- Concierge

I recently read a travel blog on *Fodors.com* forum section that stated a trip for two to Europe was averaging $12,000 per person and that was coach!

Those are a few examples of somewhat predictable events. But, what about the not-so-easy ones that sneak up on you? The ones you never saw coming? Don't worry. I have a plan.

Like any well-thought-out journey, you need to prepare for the unexpected. When planning a camping trip, it's a good idea to always take antiseptic, Band-Aids, aspirin, tweezers, and bug spray. The airlines keep those life vests on board in the unlikely event of a water landing. You must also always plan for the unlikely.

Accidents, sickness, earthquakes, floods, unemployment, death, divorce — these are just a handful of things that can rock your world. But, if you are financially prepared, I can guarantee you that the cash will help. I am not saying that you should buy an apartment building for emergency cash. What I am suggesting is that you stash a little of your cash flow away for the unlikely event of a financial *water-landing*. This is also a good conversation to have with a financial planner; risk management is high on their list of priorities. Be prepared for the unforeseen. Cash is "King" when times are tough; trust me, it's good to be the "King."

The following pages are a planning guide. Take a few minutes to journal some inner thoughts. List at least 3 or 4 items you can clearly foresee as being big expenses in your world, and then take a stab at what you guess might be a costly item or two lurking down the road.

Destination Perpetuity Planning Guide – The Known Expenses

1. _____
   _____
   _____
   _____
   _____

2. _____
   _____
   _____
   _____
   _____

3. _____
   _____
   _____
   _____
   _____

4. _____
   _____
   _____
   _____
   _____

Destination Perpetuity Planning Guide – The Unknown Expenses

1. _____
   _____
   _____
   _____
   _____
   _____

2. _____
   _____
   _____
   _____
   _____
   _____

3. _____
   _____
   _____
   _____
   _____
   _____

4. _____
   _____
   _____
   _____
   _____

Elizabeth and Howard met in their twenties. The two dated for a few months, and when Elizabeth told Howard she was pregnant, the couple decided they were meant to be together and married. After a few years passed, it became clear their marriage was amicable at best, but not fulfilling for either. When their daughter completed college and moved across the country to start a new job with her fiancé in tow, Elizabeth and Howard decided it was time for them to go their separate ways. Howard was a few years older than Elizabeth and was very settled in their home of over 20 years. Elizabeth was in her early fifties and wanted a carefree lifestyle — no yard, no pets, and lots of travel.

The couple did not hire a divorce attorney. They simple sat down one morning and discussed how to split their assets. The couple had joint savings and checking accounts. They decided that they would close the current accounts, and each partner would take 50 percent from each account. Easy.

Next up was their individual IRAs. The couple had not seen great returns, and each had a different vision for the money. They decided to leave their respective IRAs in place and not touch them unless their daughter needed money. Each of them had a pension from their individual careers, and they decided each would keep their own pension cash flow as their sole and separate incomes.

Finally was their real estate. The couple owned two properties, both free and clear. The first was their primary home, which had been dubbed "The Nest," and the second was a six-unit apartment building purchased as a safety net, which they nicknamed the "The Net." The couple called Barry, a trusted friend who was a real estate agent, and asked him about the value of the properties. Barry was familiar with both properties. He estimated the house to be worth approximately $850,000 and the apartment building to be worth approximately $925,000. The couple decided that since their daughter would inherit both properties eventually, the $75,000 difference in equity was a non-issue. They met with their CPA as to how best to transfer title without triggering a new tax basis, and within a few weeks all of their finances were separated. Elizabeth took sole title to the Net and Howard kept the Nest.

Elizabeth was excited by her newly found freedom and ready to start fresh. She had worked diligently at her job for 30 years and earned a company pension backed by her former employer. Between the cash flow of her apartment building and her pension, she planned on a very luxurious lifstyle.

She rented an apartment on the Wilshire corridor with a doorman and a view of the Hollywood Hills. Next, she leased her dream car — a convertible BMW.

After a few months of not working, Elizabeth was getting a little bored, so she spent the morning surfing the web for the best airfare deals to Spain. She found a great price on two business class seats to Madrid and called her friend Debbie to talk about booking the trip they had always imagined. Debbie said she would love to go to Spain, but she suggested Elizabeth watch the morning news before they booked the trip.

The company at which Elizabeth had worked for decades was in big trouble. Images of the CEO avoiding reporters' questions on fraud charges were playing over and over on every channel. In a relatively short time, the company Elizabeth had worked most of her adult life for folded and so did her company-backed pension.

Elizabeth was counting on her pension for her monthly bills. She had spent most of her cash on new furnishings for her apartment, her car, and a five-star ski trip. Her bills were piling up almost as fast as her savings were dwindling. Luckily she still had "The Net."

Elizabeth called her ex-husband Howard. The two met for lunch, and Howard worked out a plan for Elizabeth. Her apartment building had a newly vacated unit. If she moved in there, got rid of her Wilshire apartment, and downsized her car from an $800-a-month BMW to a $325-a-month Accord, she could afford to continue to live on her own.

The cash flow from "The Net" kept Elizabeth in a comfortable lifestyle and even got her to Madrid, in coach.

Rules of the Road

Rule #6

Expect the unexpected.

You don't have to see the top of the staircase to take the first step.

Dr. Martin Luther King

Chapter 7

Get Onboard and Stay There!

"Success in real estate starts with believing you're worthy of it."
– Matthew Ferrara

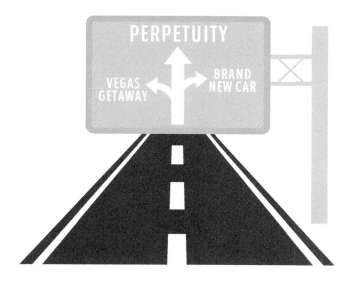

Make no mistake about it — once your assets begin to grow, you will be tested. As I've said many times before, the road to *Perpetuity* is a long one, and you will find many tempting side trails along the way, enticing you towards a seemingly quicker reward.

When you get that first mailer from a real estate agent informing you that your property is worth substantially more than you paid for it, you might be tempted to pocket the profit.

Even worse is the bank that sends you invitations for credit lines against the equity on your property. They tease and toy with your financial freedom plan with enticing temptations that tug at your every emotion and desire.

Thinking about a new car?
Ready to take that cruise around the world?
Need money for college?

Oftentimes, they will make the deal seem so attractive that you wonder how you could possibly say no.

Zero percent interest for the first three months! Wow, what a deal! Well, only if you can pay the money back in 90 days. No one ever does, and then guess what? That zero percent interest rate becomes prime plus whatever the lending institution can squeeze out of your pocket. That cheap money can get very expensive, very quickly.

Exceptions apply as we discussed in previous chapters. Life happens, and when an emergency arises, you do what you need to do with the assets that you have. But, a new red convertible is not an emergency; it is most likely a harebrained reaction of a midlife crisis. It won't make you any younger or sexier to buy that car. Staying the course and getting your cash to flow as soon as possible still won't make you younger or sexier, but it makes middle aged paunch much more palatable.

There is one exception that, depending on circumstances, I sometimes recommend. If you are in the position to pull cash from your asset while still maintaining sufficient cash flow to support the property, then it may be wise to utilize some of the increased equity to purchase another property. This is called *leveraging*.

Leveraging can be an ideal way of expanding your portfolio without exhausting your personal bank account. You are simply using the market increases in value to expand your portfolio. If such a purchase works to speed up or fatten up your goal of a perpetual stream of cash flow, then consider going for it.

Leveraging is tricky and can be dangerous, so make sure you weigh all the pros and cons with your team before traveling down that path. Your financial planner, CPA, and realtor will all have opinions. Listen to their advice, and speak to others who have built portfolios. Plan on listening a lot. Absorb information, and move forward accordingly.

The rules of the road are simple, but they are not easy to stick with. Learn them, and live by them. The peace of mind of perpetual cash flow is better than any car on the road, designer handbag, or first-class seat to Europe. Get the portfolio up and running. Then, have some fun spending it.

Tales from the Road

Travelogue #7

No Side Trips!

Christina and Ryan started investing in real estate when they were in their early twenties. Christina was a top-selling real estate broker who had an eye for good deals. Ryan worked for an airline. Together, they made a solid income, but neither of their jobs had any retirement components. Investing wisely was their only path to retirement. The couple had been diligent investors and obeyed the rules of the road. They bought properties that were distressed or poorly managed, and they turned them around. They utilized IRS 1031 to grow their portfolio and defer taxes to the future. They understood the concept of *value adds*; they knew how to improve a cap rate; and they also knew when to trade up. Their portfolio grew at a nice, slow rate.

Christina decided that the slow part was a problem. She convinced Ryan that it was time sell some of their real estate and invest in the stock market.

The couple decided to call Steven, a trusted family friend who had steered her parent's portfolio for many years. Christina and Ryan signed up with Steven and his brokerage and within a relatively short time, just as Steven had predicted, the couple's portfolio began to grow much quicker than their real estate holdings had been appreciating. The couple leveraged their income-producing property and began investing heavily in the stock and bond markets.

Some of their stock and bond portfolio were paying dividends, and they quickly re-invested those proceeds. The market began to really heat up, and the returns became intoxicating. The equity in their home had also grown nicely and in anticipation of future market growth, the couple decided to take out a second mortgage and begin remodeling their home. Soon after the remodel began, Christina found out she was pregnant. The couple was overjoyed.

The year was 2008, and much of Christina and Ryan's portfolio was connected to subprime mortgages. When Lehman Brothers crashed, so did Christina and Ryan's finances. Real estate sales slowed to a near halt, and the airline Ryan worked for began downsizing. Ryan was laid off. The remodel was costing double what the couple had budgeted, they were eating through their savings at a frightening speed, and the baby was due in a few months.

With Ryan unemployed, real estate sales evaporating, and dollars flowing out of and not into the couple's household checking account, Christina and Ryan decided to tap their $100,000 credit line on their home. When they contacted the bank to access the credit line, they found out the line of credit had been cancelled, as per the lending institution's sole prerogative. Banks were no longer giving away money. To complete the remodel, Christina and Ryan tightened their belts, sold one of their cars, cancelled the cable, and clipped coupons. They finished the house, but their finances were also finished.

Christina told me the reality of their situation hit her in a grocery store while she was standing in line to buy diapers. Both credit cards were maxed out; her ATM was declined; and there was no cash in her purse. Unable to pay, she froze with embarrassment for a moment, as did the checkout clerk and the customers behind her.

"Put those on my bill," the woman behind her said.

Christina remembers thanking the woman and leaving the store embarrassed, but also focused.

She got home and said to Ryan, "We need to sell the house."

Ryan simply nodded. It was time.

The house sold quickly, and Christina and Ryan were left with enough money to buy a new, smaller home. Instead they decided to wait. Christina knew the worst was not over yet in the real estate downturn. They rented for a while, and Christina got a new job. Ryan stayed at home with their daughter. After a few years, the couple decided the market was about to turn again. They bought in 2011 and soon after, the market caught fire. Christina went back into real estate, and within a couple of years, they were rebuilding their portfolio.

Today, they are settled into their new home and own a small apartment building they recently purchased at a great cap rate. They plan to buy one investment property every other year, if possible, until they get to six buildings with a minimum, cumulative annual positive cash flow of $100,000. In time, they will be enjoying their own *Perpetuity*, along with their wonderful daughter Sophia and new baby son Justin.

It took Christina and Ryan years to get back to where they already were before taking a side trip. The moral of the story is simple. You have a map. Use it! NO SIDE TRIPS! They are too expensive and usually not as fun as advertised, so why bother?

Rules of the Road

Rule #7

*Don't treat your investment property
like an ATM machine.*

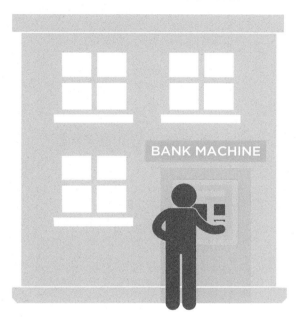

Real estate is an imperishable asset, ever increasing in value. It is the most solid security that human ingenuity has devised. It is the basis of all security and about the only indestructible security.

Russell Sage

Chapter 8

Are You *Really* Ready?

"Real estate cannot be lost or stolen, nor can it be carried away. Purchased with common sense, paid for in full, and managed with reasonable care, it is about the safest investment in the world."

– Franklin D. Roosevelt

If you have gotten this far in the book, you are clearly intrigued by the idea of building a real estate portfolio; now for the hard part. Owning income-producing real estate is a business, so let's find out if you have what it takes to buy, manage, and ultimately profit from this amazing business opportunity.

Income-producing real estate allows you to build long-term wealth by simply following the rules of the road laid out in this book. In order to truly be secure and find financial freedom you will ideally want to own more than one property. Make no mistake, you are starting a long-term business, and you should be involved at certain levels. That being said, if you have the right team in place as you build your portfolio, you will also be building systems and relationships with your team that will allow you to be less and less involved even as you acquire more property and ultimately make more money.

If you are planning on investing with a spouse or partner, sit and review the following questions together. If you are going it alone, do this exercise in a mirror. This chapter is where you get to be introspective. Income-producing real estate is a great path but not for everyone. This chapter is your opportunity to do a little journaling and really think about some of the trials that come with being a landlord. Be honest here and write down your thoughts, this information from yourself might prove the most valuable of all.

Recordkeeping is of paramount importance. Tracking your profit and loss is needed for your taxes, portfolio growth, and peace of mind.

Will I be willing to consistently keep extensive, well-organized records of all my properties, vendors, expenses, insurance, and taxes?

It takes money to make money, and if you are not willing to cough up some cash from time to time, you might want to rethink this business.

Does it make me nervous to spend money as an investment?

_____

_____

_____

_____

_____

_____

_____

_____

Risk often equals reward. Higher cap rates equal higher returns and possibly bigger headaches.

How much risk can I (and my family) tolerate?

If you are investing with a partner, then ask the additional question – Do we differ on our perception of what is risky? (If so, you might not be a good match for investing together.)

It's all about the "Benjamin's." You are walking this path to create long term cash flow, but in order to get started, you need seed money. The down payment for a real estate purchase is often the stumbling block that keeps would-be landlords out of the game. If you don't have the money, consider a partnership or a loan from Mom and Dad or transferring your 401k to a program that allows self-directed real estate investments. Getting started is the hard part, and the money is the key.

What is the source of my down payment, and can I comfortably part with those dollars?

_____

_____

_____

_____

_____

_____

_____

_____

_____

_____

Remember, this is a business, and it takes money to make money. The majority of your expenses beyond your down payment and initial purchase costs will be covered by incoming rents from your tenants; however, you will from time to time find yourself shelling out cash. You need to be ready to write a few checks now and then.

Do I have a dependable source of income to use for this investment, and how does that affect my current and future lifestyle?

Everyone's time is valuable. Regardless of whether or not you manage your properties or you have someone manage for you, there is some type of cost to you, be it time or dollars. Even if you pay to have the best property management team available overseeing your portfolio, you will still need to invest time reviewing the books and making decisions.

How many hours a week am I willing to commit to review and manage my real estate portfolio?

_____

_____

_____

_____

_____

_____

_____

_____

_____

If you choose to manage your portfolio yourself, the time you invest will be significant. Toilets break, tenants move, and when stuff happens at 3:00 a.m., your phone will ring.

Would I give up my leisure activities and a little sleep for a while to make this happen?

Time is money, and if you are a procrastinator, hire someone else to manage for you.

How often do I finish projects on time?

And if you are working with a partner ask, "Do we both approach to-do lists the same way?" and/or "Do either of us ever get frustrated with the other's procrastination?"

_____

_____

_____

_____

_____

_____

_____

_____

_____

Your travel partners are so important, and the good ones cost money. But, believe me, it is money well spent.

How willing am I to find good "partners" and pay for their counsel and heed their advice, even if it sometimes is not what I want to hear?

This can be expensive in the case of attorneys and CPAs.

Are you willing to do the heavy lifting?

Am I comfortable talking to tenants and vendors about contracts, terms, and responsibilities.

Remember, you are in this for the long haul. As your equity grows, you will be tempted to tap the cash.

Can I keep my hand out of the cookie jar and stay the course to build and grow my portfolio rather than tapping my equity and grabbing short-term returns?

Owning income-producing real estate is a business, and you must treat it as such. If you are really ready, then do not hesitate. Get on the path.

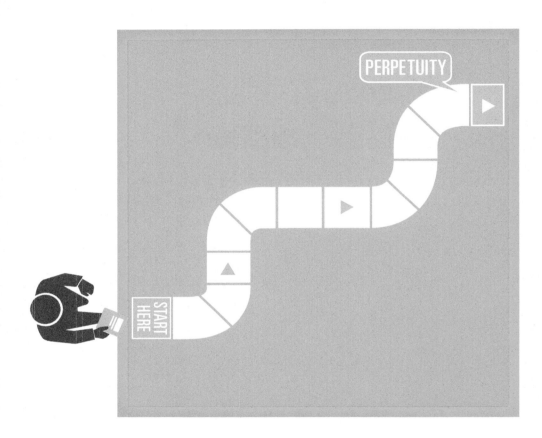

Twenty years ago, I had a client named Jason. He had just moved to southern California from upstate New York. On Jason's 30th birthday, he and his twin brother Jasper were given an amazing opportunity. Their parents offered each of them $50,000 towards the purchase of their first home.

Jasper wasted no time and was under contract for a home within two weeks of the offer. Jason was reluctant about the idea of homeownership, but his trusted twin Jasper encouraged him not to miss out. Jason and I set out a few days later to find his first home. We looked at everything on the market for several weeks, and although we found a few suitable properties, Jason finally decided homeownership was not for him.

"Why?" I asked.

"I really like my freedom." Jason replied.

I then peppered the conversation with all of the financially sound reasons to buy real estate, not the least of which was his parent's offer to give him the down payment.

"I already told my dad I'm out for now, and he said the offer will be good when I'm ready."

A few months later Jason met Mark, the man of his dreams, and the two moved to Hawaii. After Jason moved, he and I exchanged a few Christmas cards, but after a couple of years, we lost touch.

Years later, I ran into Jason by chance in an airport. We both had a little time before our flights, and we caught up over a cup of coffee. Jason told me that he and Mark had lived in Hawaii for a few years, but ultimately settled in Seattle. I asked if he had ever taken his parents up on the offer of the down payment on a home.

"No," he said. "One of my biggest mistakes was not buying a place when I had the chance."

Jason told me that his father's seemingly solid financial position had melted down rather quickly when he discovered his business partner had been embezzling. Jason explained that his father's former business partner leveraged most of the company's holdings into a series of bad investments. Then, when it became apparent that he could not pay the debt back, he syphoned off all the remaining cash before disappearing. Since Jason's father owned the company 50/50 with the former partner, his father decided to do the right thing and sold off what he could salvage from the company. He then used most of his personal assets to pay back investors and the remaining debts. Jason's father avoided any lawsuits but was left with very little in the way of personal wealth. To make matters worse, Jason's mother had died last year, and now his father was showing signs of early Alzheimer's. His doctor recommended that he enter a care facility. Jason's brother Jasper had three children, and he and his wife both worked full time, leaving the couple little to no discretionary time or income to put towards their father's care. Jason and Mark would be covering the responsibility on their own.

Jason lamented the offer his father had made so many years ago.

"I wish I had taken my dad up on the down payment to buy a place. My brother was the smart one. His mortgage is nothing. I really should have bought when I had the chance. The care facility for my dad is crazy expensive. I doubt I will ever be able to buy a home now. Woulda, shoulda, coulda."

As you might imagine, I had a few thoughts to share on the subject of his future ability to buy a home, and we spent our last few minutes discussing his current family and financial situation. I mapped out a few ideas as to how he and Mark could afford to get into the real estate market. I suggested Jason speak with a real estate agent I knew in Seattle. Jason and I finished our coffee and headed for our respective flights, promising this time to stay in touch.

I recently received an email from Jason that he and Mark were doing well and had settled into their new home. In the email, Jason explained that he had worked with the agent I suggested and he laid out a plan for using Jason's income as well as his father's social security income to create a blended household where Jason's father could live with Jason and Mark as opposed to a care facility. The numbers worked and so did the living situation.

I received a Christmas card from Jason last year showing all three of them in horrendously bad Christmas sweaters in front of a roaring fireplace.

Jason scribbled across the front just three words — *Home at Last!*

Rules of the Road

Rule #8

When opportunity knocks, answer!

Ask not that the journey be easy; ask instead that it be worth it.

John Fitzgerald Kennedy

Chapter 9
Building Your Portfolio

"If you don't own a home, buy one. If you own a home, buy another one. If you own two homes, buy a third. And lend your relatives the money to buy a home."

– John Paulson

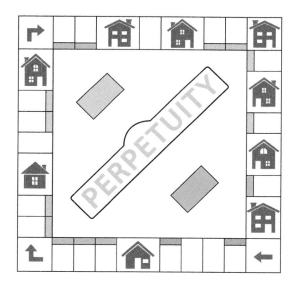

At the beginning of this book, I made the claim that I would show you how to create a lifetime of perpetual income. The road has been mapped out, but like all journeys, it is now up to you to take that first step and arguably hardest step.

When my parents first decided to build a real estate portfolio they did not have a lot of money, but they did have a clear focus. They wanted a safe, secure stream of cash flow that they could count on for as long as they needed to. They did their homework, studied the rental histories of potential properties, reviewed the comparable sales in the area, and sought the counsel of all the appropriate professionals before selecting and purchasing properties. They made careful, intelligent purchases. They maintained their properties and allowed a qualified property manager to handle all the day-to-day aspects of management while keeping informed so that they could make the major decisions along the way. Their plan was plotted cautiously and executed thoughtfully. Their portfolio was not large, just a few properties, and it took them over a decade to build. There were times when money got tight, especially just after a purchase, but in the long run, each property they acquired did exactly what it was intended to do. And when it was time to slow down and reap the fruits of their labor, the cash flowed, and my parents enjoyed the good life. They traveled, spent freely, and lived comfortably.

Once you have your feet wet with your first property, chances are those passive income checks will make you hungry for more. It's hard to retire off of just one property, and in my opinion, it is also risky. Once you have acquired your first property, the task of building a portfolio will seem much less daunting.

Building a portfolio is not as complicated as it might sound, but it does take time, preparation, and money. Once you have set up your team with a real estate agent that knows how to sniff out deals and a property management company that knows how to drive cash flow, the only issue left is how to finance your continued purchases.

There are different ways to fund additional properties with which to build a portfolio. If you have discretionary cash lying around, the down payment is easy. But, what if you don't have any extra funds, then what? Most people without access to a wealthy and generous relative need to be creative. Since everyone's situation is unique, you will need to discuss what strategy is best for your situation with your financial planner, CPA, lender, and of course your trusted real estate agent.

Here are a few ideas about how to continue the journey and grab a few more properties along the way:

Set aside your cash flow profits for the down payment on your next property.

The best way to build a portfolio is by not spending the proceeds too soon or too frivolously. Set up a bank account, and let any excess funds grow. It takes time and money to build a portfolio; the Porsche can wait.

Remember to set aside some money not just to grow the portfolio, but also a little rainy day cash. I typically keep a cash reserve of around six months' worth of expenses for each property. I know other investors who are comfortable with as little as three months' worth and some who would never think of having less than 12 months' worth of cash on hand. Know your property, understand your risks, and gauge your own level of tolerance.

Is leveraging my current income-producing property to buy more property a good idea?

Many real estate agents and lenders would answer, "Yes!" to this question. My answer is, "Not so fast." Remember, one of the first rules of the road is, **no detours**. Before taking a dime out of your property, take a long hard look at the financial strength of that asset. Ask yourself these questions first:

- Do I have strong cash reserves on hand for maintenance, vacancy, and emergencies?

- How will leveraging my asset affect the cash flow? Whatever amount you pull out will undoubtedly increase your existing mortgage payment and will thereby lessen your cash flow.

TRAVEL TIP

Getting your financial team together might appear daunting but trust me, a well-planned 10-to 15-minute conference call is typically a great way to iron out all the pros and cons quickly and allow you to make informed decisions with multiple view points. I have found these quick calls can often create an informed and intelligent consensus in a very short time.

Be very careful with leveraging. This can be one of the most hazardous side trips you can take. It can also be one of the most lucrative and one of the best ways to grow your portfolio. Leverage is all about timing. When your asset has gained enough equity to borrow funds without jeopardizing the property, it might be time to leverage a portion of the equity.

The proper use of leveraging can bump your retirement trip to Hawaii from sticky coach seats with paper cups to a first-class voyage of supple leather loungers with crystal champagne flutes. Just be careful with this one. Taking a wrong turn can cause you to veer off your own fiscal cliff.

Can I use my IRA or 401K to invest in property?

Maybe. Some IRAs will now let you self-direct into real estate. If your provider does not allow for such investments, you can sometimes move your IRA or 401K to a provider that does allow for self-directed real estate investments. Before making such a move, look and see how your IRA or 401K portfolios have been doing compared to your income-producing real estate. Compare the equity gains and the cash flow along with risk and volatility. Oftentimes, income-producing real estate fairs far better, but each investor needs to review this on an individual basis. Leave your realtor and financial planner out of the initial conversation, and first review the pros and cons with your CPA. He or she will be a good, non-biased second set of eyes for this comparison. This is a complicated process, so again be careful here, and double check all the rules with your appropriate travel companions.

What about partnerships?

I have found partnering with trusted friends and family members can be both lucrative and maddening. Having said that, it can also be a shortcut to building a portfolio. Why? Simply because you can acquire more property in less time and build equity faster while spreading out the risk. Think of it this way. If you have

$100,000, you can put it all down on one property, or you can create partnerships, still investing $100,000 total as a down payment, but you invest $50,000 into two properties. Your investment is still $100,000, but now your risk is shared and thereby lessened. Arguably, you have increased your growth potential on your investments since several small equity stakes can sometimes help to grow your portfolio faster as you are not tied to only one building in one area of growth.

You still have to do your homework and be very thoughtful before investing with friends or family. Even if it is your best friend or your twin sister, make sure everything is in writing. The issue is not so much trust, but clarity.

Be careful here; the best of friends and the closest of family members can come to ruinous ends when things are not carefully spelled out. People's goals and finances change, some die, and others sometimes just go nuts. All of these scenarios and so many more can drastically change the original intention of the partnership. Make sure you have clear contracts and written understandings with delegations of duties, outlined distribution and contribution schedules, ownership rights, and exit strategies.

Is seller financing a good option?

One of the greatest challenges of buying income property can be the down payment. Depending on the property, banks often want 30 percent or more as a down payment for income-producing properties. You might consider asking the seller to *carry paper* to help finance the loan for the first few years. The terms of these *seller carry* sales vary, but typically the interest rate is similar to the banks. If the seller is open to seller financing, this can be a win-win, with the buyer getting help with lending requirements of the acquisition and the seller getting a good return on the borrowed money.

Is a 1031 exchange the right move?

Remember the first rule of the road: *Never sell anything!* But, by all means feel free to *trade*.

We touched on this earlier in the book, but lets get a little more in depth. When done correctly, 1031 tax exchanges are one of the most lucrative opportunities for growing your portfolio while deferring your tax liabilities. Ask your agent to monitor your properties and the market conditions annually. If your agent is on top of the market, he or she can guide you through trades when the market is right. A good real estate agent can create an ever-increasing income stream simply by guiding you with a series of trades and growing your portfolio via equity increases and market movement. Make sure you consult with a 1031 intermediary and CPA before making any moves here.

Remember the 1031 time frames. The IRS does not give grace periods. Adhering to the 1031 tax exchange rules can defer substantial tax liabilities throughout much if not your entire lifetime. Not being mindful of the time periods and other various 1031 rules can cost you greatly. Pay attention here. The Internal Revenue Service is giving you a gift by allowing the deferment of taxes; however, the IRS does not mess around if you do not obey the rules.

Like all successful journeys, the planning stage takes time. Be patient with the process. Real estate investing is a long road, and proper planning is the key. Hard work and forgoing some of life's more extravagant pleasures may be required while you build your portfolio, but the end result can be a comfortable, safe, secure, lifestyle with steady cash flow. By following the simple steps outlined in this book, you can make that goal a reality. Remember the rules of the road, and keep this book handy. Refer to the notes you took. Once you own your properties, the key to success becomes what I call the three M's:

- **Management** — If you have the right management team in place, your building should keep a high occupancy rate and retain a steady cash flow.

- **Maintenance** — If you maintain your property and get ahead of maintenance issues before they become huge problems, you will save yourself time, money, and headaches.

- **Monitoring** — Monitoring your property means knowing your property, the market, and the competition. Be sure you know:

    - The current market rents in your area
    - The value of your property
    - Your cap rate
    - If your area is improving , languishing, or degrading
    - How long you have on the depreciation schedule
    - Your current interest rates and when it's time to refinance
    - Your equity position, and make sure your money is getting a proper market return

Your real estate agent and your management company can help out with the monitoring, but you will need to continually ask the right questions. Put a reminder in your calendar to contact your realtor every year on the anniversary of your purchase to do an annual comparative market analysis. Ask your property manager to do a biannual rent assessment of the area. Know when to raise the rent, and know if it is time to move the asset; plan when and how you will grow your portfolio, and prepare to be flexible.

Let me wrap up this book with one final example of why I think income-producing real estate is by far your best bet investment for a long-term, perpetual cash flow return. I like to break things down to simplified views. The way I see it, every investment has three stages: A beginning, middle and an end. Simple.

The first step is always the same, regardless of what path you choose, stocks, bonds, precious metals, real estate or any other type of investment you must first commit to an investment strategy and then personally shell out some cash.

The second step is a continued funding of your investment. In order to grow an asset to a point where you can take distributions, the venture must be continually funded. With stocks and bonds, your broker will encourage you to buy more shares every month and will most likely suggest you set up an automatic monthly withdrawals from your checking account to build up your portfolio. This is a necessary step in growing most any type of investment. These dollars will need to come directly out of your pocket.

Here is where real estate first begins to shine. When you own income-producing real estate, the majority of the continued funding of your asset will come in the form of rents from your tenants. If you follow the rules of the road laid out in this book the mortgage, taxes, insurance, maintenance, and most other associated costs should be paid almost entirely by your tenants. Now, that is not to say you may not have out-of-pocket expenses from time to time; you most likely will; however, the majority of the continued funding of your asset will be paid by your tenants, not you.

The third stage is the best. The distribution. Most investment plans have a dispersal strategy. At a certain point in time, the investor begins taking allocations from the investment. With stocks, bonds, precious metals, and most other types of investments, when you begin taking distributions you also begin diminishing the asset itself. Stocks, bonds, and mutual funds will need to be sold and cashed out to put dollars in your pocket. The longer you live, the less your asset is worth, and the hope is you don't out live your money. With real estate, the distributions you will be receiving comes from the rents your tenants pay. An income-producing real estate portfolio, planned and executed correctly, should grow to a point that allows the excess rents to come directly into your personal bank account. The same rents that went to pay off the mortgage should land directly in your wallet. And unlike other investments in which the asset itself must be sold off to fund your monthly allocations, the real estate you own (the actual asset) should never be touched but rather left whole to appreciate even as it continues to distribute excess cash flow month after month, year after year, and decade after decade.

Now for the added bonus. Your real estate portfolio of financial freedom can be handed down to your children, your grandchildren, or left to your favorite charity. This is what I call generational investing.

The rule of Perpetuity

This book is filled with rules and warnings to heed them but there is one rule I want to break. It's called the rule of 25. Financial institutions have used what they call the 25% rule to help investors build a retirement plan. The formula is simple. For example lets say an investor decides he or she will need $5,000 a month in order to retire and wants to begin retirement at age 65. Based on the 25% rule the investor will need 25 times $5,000 or $1,250,000 in order to retire.

Once the investor reaches 65, 4% of the accumulated retirement funds are distributed annually. This plan has been around for years and it works fairly well but there is one major flaw. What if you live longer than 25 years, then what? With income generated from real estate as your monthly allocation, your cash continues regardless of how long you live. The last thing you want to be is 90 years old and broke.

As I stated in the beginning of the book I chose the title Destination Perpetuity because one of the definitions of Perpetuity is "An annuity without end."

How long will you live? Since no one can answer that question I think its time to rewrite the rules. Lets replace the Rule of 25 with the Rule of Perpetuity.

So let's recap the advantages of income-producing real estate:

- Inflation friendly
- Safe, secure
- Potential asset growth during distributions
- Nearly recession proof
- Multiple IRS / tax incentives
- Continually funded by your tenants
- A legacy to make sure your heirs speak kindly of you

I personally don't know of any better investment. It's not quick, and it's not easy, but it works. I watched my parents build their portfolio, and then I built portfolios for my clients and my family. Now, it's your turn.

In the late 1980s, I scraped together every dime I had, and along with two friends, Cindy and Sean, I purchased my first piece of investment real estate. I was 26. The property consisted of two, tiny houses on one big lot in a suburb of San Diego. The rents covered the majority of our mortgage, taxes, insurance, and maintenance.

A few years later, I purchased my first primary residence, a condo in Hermosa Beach, California. I held both properties through a market cycle and saw a dramatic upturn in real estate values; both properties had taken a nice ride on the equity train. I began building my portfolio by utilizing the IRS 1031 tax exchange and traded my San Diego property for an income property with better cash flow. I then refinanced my primary residence and pulled cash from my equity-rich Hermosa Beach property to begin increasing my portfolio via leveraging. I was on the path. I started with a small fix-and-flip and then reinvested into duplexes and triplexes. I moved into larger properties. Next up was a five-unit building, followed by an eight-unit building. Then came a 15-unit building, and then a 22-unit building. My portfolio was growing nicely, and I was on the road to *Perpetuity*.

But then I took a side trip. With a hot stock market, I refinanced and pulled out cash to buy *can't miss* stocks. Then, I ventured into tenants-in-common portfolio deals run by a company with an amazing track record. The stock market failed as did my stockbroker's *can't miss* picks. Worse yet, the tenant-in-common company I had invested heavily in turned out to be a Ponzi scheme. My *side trip* cost me more money than I care to admit and set me back at least a decade. I knew the rules, but I thought I could bend them. Never again.

Follow the simple *Rules of the Road* laid out in this book, and then sit back and wait for the equity train to arrive. Given time, rents go up, values go up, and so do your profits. Success will be yours if you simply stay on the path and remember to keep the ultimate goal in mind. Cash flow for life. An annuity without end.

Rules of the Road

Rule #9

Enjoy Perpetuity.

The major fortunes in America have been made in land.

John D. Rockefeller

About The Author:

Craig O'Rourke has worked in the real estate industry full time as a sales agent, Branch Manager, and coach since 1992. Specializing in income producing real estate, Craig has helped hundreds of clients achieve their dreams of financial freedom by building real estate portfolios and creating *mailbox income*.

During his time as a Branch Manager, Craig oversaw the daily operations of two flagship Coldwell Banker offices managing hundreds of millions of dollars in sales every year.

As a real estate sales coach, Craig has taught other industry professionals how to build, maintain and grow real estate portfolios.

In his sales career, Craig has personally represented several hundred clients in every facet of the real estate industry including commercial, residential, investment and ground up development. Craig has also served on the Greater Los Angeles Presidents Counsel as an advisor to the President of Coldwell Banker and currently he is working on two new real estate books, one entitled "The Rule of Perpetuity" and the other entitled "What Now, What Next?"

Craig O'Rourke has consistently ranked among the top real estate agents both locally and nationally for two decades and has received numerous top sales awards including Coldwell Banker's prestigious Presidents Award.

Craig resides in Redondo Beach, California with his partner Andrew, son Tyler and dog Clooney.

CPSIA information can be obtained
at www.ICGtesting.com
Printed in the USA
FSOW04n1600261017
40351FS